MW01248153

Repair Your Credit and Knock Out Your Debt

Repair Your Credit and Knock Out Your Debt

Jeff Michael
Thom Fox

McGraw-Hill

New York   Chicago   San Francisco   Lisbon
London   Madrid   Mexico City   Milan
New Delhi   San Juan   Seoul   Singapore
Sydney   Toronto

The **McGraw·Hill** *Companies*

Copyright © 2004 by Jeff Michael and Springboard. All rights reserved. Printed in the United States of America. Except as permitted under the United States Copyright Act of 1976, no part of this publication may be reproduced or distributed in any form or by any means, or stored in a data base or retrieval system, without the prior written permission of the publisher.

1 2 3 4 5 6 7 8 9 0 DOC/DOC 0 9 8 7 6 5 4

ISBN 0-07-142613-2

McGraw-Hill books are available at special quantity discounts to use as premiums and sales promotions, or for use in corporate training programs. For more information, please write to the Director of Special Sales, McGraw-Hill Professional, Two Penn Plaza, New York, NY 10121-2298. Or contact your local bookstore.

 This book is printed on recycled, acid-free paper containing a minimum of 50% recycled, de-inked fiber.

Library of Congress Cataloging-in-Publication Data

Michael, Jeff.
    Repair your credit and knock out your debt / by Jeff Michael.
        p.   cm.
    Includes bibliographical references.
    ISBN 0-07-142613-2 (alk. paper)
    1. Consumer credit. 2. Debt. 3. Finance, Personal. I. Title.
HG3755.M49 2004
332.024'02—dc22

                                            2003023692

Contents

Foreword

Defending the U.S. Credit System

There are some who might argue that the credit system in our country is broken. With bankruptcy on the rise, and Americans borrowing more and saving less, it could be argued that we have lost our way.

While it's certainly true that our nation is increasingly dependent on credit and debt, that doesn't mean that the system itself is broken. If consumer confidence is the engine that drives our economy, credit transactions are where the wheels meet the road. The U.S. credit system, far from being broken, is essential to the greatness of our economic system.

The answer to America's problems with credit isn't legislation or an overhaul of the consumer credit system; it lies within each of us. Education and self-examination are the keys to decreasing our overreliance on credit and becoming a nation of savers.

The problem isn't easy access to credit; our free society offers us a number of choices when we seek to borrow. The far more pressing problem is that we as a people have put the accumulation of money and status at the forefront of our culture. Our values are tied to material wealth instead of to what's really important: our relationships with our families and loved ones.

That's the downside of our great economic system: Capitalism has encouraged rampant consumerism, and there is great temptation to spend money that we don't have. And unfortunately, easy access to credit gives us the ready means to do just that.

The greatest change we can make is to revisit our priorities, realize what's really important, and make smart decisions about our individual borrowing.

Until then, nonprofit agencies like Springboard are here to help consumers who fear they've gotten in too deep. Over 14,000 consumers call us each month, and we're only one agency out of thousands.

Springboard Non-Profit Consumer Credit Management has been in business for nearly 30 years, helping consumers in southern California and all over the nation to repay their debt and avoid bankruptcy. This book represents a small portion of the combined experience and knowledge of our agency, as related by two writers: our director of education, Jeff Michael, and the talented young novelist Thom Fox.

We're especially excited to have Thom involved in this book, and not just because he's such a good writer. Thom, like 65 million other American households, found himself so deep in debt that he was having trouble getting by. His firsthand experience with debt, combined with Jeff's expertise, has informed every page of this book.

The unique thing about this project is that the book is only part of the picture. Springboard offers free, confidential counseling on demand to consumers all over the country. All it takes is a phone call to 1-800-WISE-PLAN (1-800-947-3752) or a visit to our web site (www.credit.org) to get started.

Dianne Wilkman
President/CEO
Springboard Non-Profit Consumer Credit Management

Chapter 1

Knowing Where to Start

DON'T DESPAIR! WHY IT IS POSSIBLE TO SUCCESSFULLY CONQUER YOUR DEBTS

Most books about getting out of debt or improving one's credit begin with a lengthy section along the lines of "how to know if you've got debt trouble."

We're going to dispense with that section in this book.

The fact is, if you picked up this book, you're looking for help. These days, who doesn't have problems with mounting debt? Our guess is that you don't need 40 pages to help you deduce that you're in trouble. We're going to cut right to the heart of the matter.

First, let us quickly reassure you: It is possible to knock out your debt and turn your situation around, no matter how dire that situation may be.

One of the coauthors of this book, Jeff Michael, is the director of education at Springboard Non-Profit Consumer Credit Management. At Springboard, we see just about everything. We see working mothers who are as paralyzed by $1500 of debt as someone else is by being $300,000 in the hole.

We also get calls from people who are truly at the end of their rope—people who fear that things will never improve and think that suicide may be their only answer.

We hope you don't feel that way, but whatever your situation, don't despair. You can overcome your debt. Remember, there are no debtors' prisons in the United States. You're not the only person with debt, either. Consider these statistics:

- There are 185 million American consumers with credit cards.
- Some 150 million new lines of credit were opened last year in the United States.
- The average credit card debt in America is $8400.

And that's just credit cards—that doesn't include auto loans, consumer loans, mortgages, student loans, and so on. The fact is, debt is a way of life in our country. You're not alone, and if all of those other people can stick with it, so can you.

If you do feel that things have gotten hopeless, if thoughts of suicide have crossed your mind, then you need to pick up the phone. You'll need more than a book like this has to offer. Talk to a living, breathing person before you do anything drastic.

But if you're ready to tackle your debt, then read on. Springboard and organizations like it have helped thousands of consumers conquer their financial woes, and this book will help you use our principles and techniques to help yourself.

WHERE TO START: THE THINGS YOU SHOULD DO RIGHT NOW

Take a deep breath—we're starting.

Your road to financial freedom begins right now. This is not the kind of thing that you should take a few weeks or even days to think about. If you're serious about overcoming your debt, you have to make the commitment and jump in.

Why? Because it's not easy, and every day you delay it, it gets even harder.

For example, when you're planning to go on a diet, what's the first thing you do?

You eat. Think about it. It's Thursday, and your great new diet starts, you've decided, on Monday. That gives you one last weekend of freedom—freedom to eat whatever you want. So Friday through Sunday is a

3-day binge of all the stuff you're absolutely going to swear off of on Monday. Is that healthy? Does it work out in the long run? Of course not.

Like going on a diet, changing your financial situation means making the commitment and going for it. We're about to tell you to cut up your credit cards. That's right. And when we do, you've got to do it now. Don't plan to do it next week, because we know there are things you want to run out and buy with those cards before you destroy them. Don't give yourself the weekend to max that card out. Just cut it up.

This brings us to some immediate steps you should take as you're getting started.

- *Stop incurring new debt.* You'll never get out of debt by borrowing more money. Before this chapter is done, you're going to assess your debt situation, and we can't have you mucking up the process by continuing to borrow.

    The first step in this process is—you guessed it—to cut up your credit cards.

    You don't have to cancel your accounts. In fact, it will probably be better for your credit rating in the long run if you keep the accounts open. What you will do, though, is stop charging to those accounts.

    Go ahead and do it. You can always order a new card if you decide to quit. It's just plastic, after all.

- *Live on a cash basis.* Get used to this idea right now. Until your debt is under control, you're going to be buying everything with cash.

    It's not that difficult, and it'll get easier and easier. Once you've achieved financial freedom, we'll teach you to use credit cards wisely, and you can reenter the world of credit better prepared.

    But until then, buy things only if you've got the cash for them. That will mean saving up for some things and setting goals, a subject that we'll tackle in a few pages.

- *Get a handle on your situation.* Sit down with all your paperwork. Gather your bills, statements, everything relating to your debt. Make sure everything is as current as possible. It may be helpful to have a copy of your credit report handy so that you can include any old debts that are listed there. (See Chapter 6 for information on how to obtain your credit report.)

Add up your total debt first. You want as complete a picture as possible of what you owe (see Figure 1-1).

You want to identify what you owe and to whom, and what your monthly payments are and when they're due.

What you come up with may shock you. You may be over-whelmed, or you may be pleasantly surprised. Either way, realize that thousands of consumers have conquered debt with our help, and they all started just like this.

Once you've assessed your debt situation and gotten it all down on paper, you've taken control of it. You now have it in a fixed form; you know the amount you owe, and you're ready to knock it out.

- *Prepare a budget.* Chapter 2 is all about budgeting. Whatever method you use, you've got to create a budget if you want to be debt-free. You may hear people talk about a "spending plan," which is really just a touchy-feely way of saying budget. The thinking is that people hate to hear the word *budget*, that budgets don't work, and so on.

  But budgets do work if you do them right, and if it helps you, go ahead and think of what you're preparing as a spending plan. Because that's all a budget is: a plan for how you're going to spend your money.

- *Relax.* Take it one day at a time. You're not going to get out of debt overnight, and you're going to have some difficulties. That's okay. There will be days when you can't take it anymore and you'll run to the mall and splurge. You'll bust your budget from time to time. All of this is fine as long as you don't give up. If you fall off the horse, get back on and keep riding. That's good advice in this or any situation.

THINKING LONG-TERM

As we prepare to talk about setting goals, we can't stress enough the importance of long-term thinking.

Figure 1-1 Charting Out Your Debt

Name of Creditor	Total Amount Owed	Monthly Payment	Interest Rate	Date Due Each Month

Total Debt: _____

Total Monthly Payments: _____

As we just said, this isn't an overnight process, and you have to keep your eye on your destination. It'll be a few years before you completely emerge from debt, but by then you'll be in better financial shape than ever, controlling your spending and living on a cash basis. And your credit will be in great shape, too.

The flip side of long-term thinking is what it's costing you to wait. For example, think long-term when it comes to purchases. If you buy a $2000 big-screen TV, chances are you're going to pay a lot more than $2000.

Most of us would make that kind of purchase on a credit card, and that means we'll be paying interest. We'll take a closer look at how credit and interest work later, but for now, take a look at this math:

> You pay $2000 for that big-screen TV on a credit card that charges 20 percent interest. You then pay the minimum monthly payment of 2 percent of the balance without ever charging another dime to the card. That debt ends up taking more than 40 years to pay off and costing you more than $8000 in interest. That means the $2000 TV you bought on credit cost you over $10,000. Was it worth it?

Now let's turn that around. Let's say you take the same $2000, now in cash, and you put it into an IRA for 50 years. With 8 percent interest, you'd end up with over $100,000.

The point here is to think long-term. The important things you do in your life—buying a car, buying a house, getting a college education, raising kids—all require some long-term commitment. Add conquering your debt to that list, make it a priority, and you'll be a long way toward making the mental adjustment necessary to achieve financial freedom.

THE THREE TYPES OF GOALS

A big part of the process is setting goals and working to attain them. Your overall goal is to become debt-free. Along the way, you'll set smaller, more readily obtainable goals.

This is crucial. One of the key distinctions we see between those people who are generally successful in life and those who aren't is that successful people set goals for themselves. This applies to all aspects of life, not just getting out of debt. Always have a plan for where you want to be a year from now, 3 years from now, 20 years from now. These things may change and evolve as time goes by, and that's okay, but you've got to set a destination before you start your journey.

- *Short-term goals.* We define a short-term goal as anything that takes less than 1 year to achieve.

    We're talking money management now, so let's think in financial terms. Say you want to take a trip to Las Vegas. (We advise against gambling, as it promotes financial irresponsibility, so we're assuming that you're only going for the entertainment, right?) You want to go at this time next year, and (to make the math easy) you need $1200 for the trip. You simply need to save $100 per month over the course of the year, and your trip is paid for.

    It's that easy. You can even break it down to a paycheck basis. When you're done, you've got the money to go on the trip, and you can leave the credit cards and even the ATM card behind so that there's no danger of your overspending. You've got a nice, guilt-free vacation, paid for in advance. Remember that you have to work before you get paid, and setting short-term goals makes you earn these luxuries.
- *Intermediate goals.* These goals take between 1 and 5 years to achieve.

    Saving up for a car, perhaps saving for the down payment on a house—these are good mid-range goals. You figure them just the way you do the short-term goals, but they'll take longer, and we're dealing with larger amounts of money (see Figure 1-2).

    Your plan to conquer debt may be an intermediate goal. Certainly you want to have your credit card debt wiped out in less than 5 years. If you've got a large amount of student loan debt or a 30-year mortgage, then you won't be completely debt-free in 5 years. But you can wipe out the most expensive and least beneficial debt, and that means paying off that plastic.
- *Long-term goals.* Any goal more than 5 years away is a long-term goal.

    Saving for a college education, saving for retirement, paying off your mortgage—a long-term goal has to become part of your

Figure 1-2 Goals

Financial Goals	Target Date	Total Needed	Current Savings	Additional Savings Needed	# of Pay Periods Until Target Date	Savings Needed Per Pay Period	Savings Needed per Month
Example: A New Car	36 months	$20,650	$6,250	$14,400	72	200	400
Short-Term Goals							
Intermediate Goals							
Long-Term Goals							

life for the foreseeable future. You'll be socking money away from here on out if you want to achieve these goals. And you'd better, because these are the most important.

SIX KEY COMPONENTS OF A GOOD GOAL

1. *Concrete.* It can't be nebulous. "Peace on Earth" might be a good goal for society, but for you, something like "to be fulfilled" simply won't do the trick. Figure out what you want in a way that you can define concretely. "I want to be completely debt-free and have good credit" is your goal.

2. *Achievable.* "I want to be a millionaire" might be a concrete goal, but is it realistic? Some of us can hope to get there in our lifetimes, but it's hard to say how attainable that kind of goal is for each individual.

   You may feel that you will never achieve your goal of being debt-free; if you're over $60,000 in debt just on credit cards, you may want to give up. Don't. We help people with more debt than that all the time.

3. *Measurable.* We're dealing with personal finance, so it's easy to set measurable goals. We've already had you assess your debt situation, so you should have a good sense of where you stand.

   This should get even easier as your goals get smaller. If you just want to pay off that Visa card with the $5000 balance, then you have a concrete, measurable goal, and one that you can track in detail. You'll be able to say, "I'm 20 percent of the way there," and when you're down to $2500, you can say, "I'm halfway there." This kind of measurability is a great help in achieving the goals you set for yourself.

4. *Self-determined.* "I want to win the lottery," is not a goal. It's a dream. Your goals should have outcomes that you can affect.

5. *Consistent.* Your goals can't be mutually exclusive. "I want to be completely free from credit card debt within 4 years" probably isn't compatible with "I want to have a completely new wardrobe exclusively from Saks Fifth Avenue." Sometimes you'll have to

achieve one goal before you can work on another. And since you're reading a book on getting out of debt, we're making that your top priority.

6. *Targeted.* You need an end date for your goals. "I want to pay off my credit cards" isn't sufficient. The credit card companies have that same goal for you; they just want it to take 30 years. You need to take a look at your finances and see how quickly you can eliminate your debt. When consumers come to Springboard Non-Profit Consumer Credit Management for counseling, we usually advise a debt repayment plan that takes around 4 years.

YOUR FIRST GOAL: THE EMERGENCY SAVINGS FUND

We've already decided that your larger goal is "to become debt-free and have good credit." But you'll need to achieve a lot of smaller goals in order to get there.

Your first goal is this: You must build up an emergency savings fund that equals 3 months' income within the next 12 months.

"Wait a minute," you're saying. "If I were capable of saving 3 months' income, why would I need help?"

Virtually every financial expert will tell you how important the emergency savings fund is, and virtually every consumer will have your reaction.

But the truth is, you *are* capable of saving 3 months' worth of income, and you're going to have to. Because until you have that emergency savings fund in place, you're never truly secure.

Imagine being able to live for 90 days without needing any money coming in. Three months is a long time, and it should be ample to correct your situation if you experience, for example, sudden unemployment.

Again, you're not going to meet this goal overnight. You have to look at your finances, read Chapter 2 and complete a budget, and see how much money you can set aside every month for your emergency savings fund. We'll give you some guidelines on how to do it. Trust us, it is possible, and you shouldn't have to fundamentally change your personality in order to do it.

CREATING AN ACTION PLAN FOR FINANCIAL FREEDOM

When we counsel clients at Springboard Non-Profit Consumer Credit Management, we help them prepare a budget and give them an action plan that can help them achieve some of their goals.

What you need to do is create an action plan for yourself. We'll get you started right here, but to complete your plan, you may have to use all the chapters of this book.

Let's take a look at a typical client action plan (see Figure 1-3).

As you can see, we start by determining the client's root concern. Budgeting, credit use, overspending—there are certain common things we hear when we are trying to ascertain the reasons for a client's financial situation. Here's how our clients break down when asked why they sought credit counseling:

35% No budget
21% Reduced income
15% Unemployment
10% Illness
4% Divorce
3% Caring for relative or friend
2% Death in the family
2% Marriage expenses
2% Gambling
2% Military service
4% Other

As you can see, budgeting is the number-one issue. Too many of us operate without any plan for our money, and it gets us into lots of trouble.

Our counselors help the client create a budget during the counseling session, and the basic numbers are represented on the action plan. If there's a deficit, we work with the consumer to come up with ideas on how to make up the deficit.

Then we propose solutions, breaking down the client's future actions into clear steps. No two action plans are alike. What you'll have to do is use

Figure 1-3   Client Action Plan

SPRINGBOARD
NON-PROFIT CONSUMER CREDIT MANAGEMENT

Client Action Plan

Client Name: _____ Joe Client _____   Counselor Name: _____ Mary Counselor _____
Co-Client: _____

Client's Financial Concern:

☐ Budgeting and Money Management   ☑ Credit Report Status

☑ Credit Use   ☑ Debt Repayment

☐ Mortgage Delinquency   ☐ Overspending

☐ Other _____

Budget Assessment Summary:

	Proposed Through DMP	Source of Funds to Make Up Deficit
Total Monthly Net Income	$ 1,850	REDUCE EXPENSES; GET A ROOMMATE
Less Minimum Monthly Living Expenses	- $ 1,653	
Less Debt Repayment Amount	- $ 205	
Budget Surplus (Deficit)	= ($8)	

Client's Proposed Financial Solution:

☐ Full Time Employment   ☐ Spouse's Employment

☐ Additional Employment   ☑ Housing Options

☐ Sell Automobile/Refinance   ☐ Sale/Liquidate Assets

☑ Implement Budget/Reduce Expenses   ☐ Liquidate/Reduce Savings/Investments

☐ Other _____   ☐ Tax Refund

Action Steps:

1. Look for ways to reduce expenses (see www.credit.org and www.worldshare.org)
2. Attend "Power of Paycheck Planning" and "Road Map To Financial Freedom" Seminars
3. Get a rommate to help with cost of housing
4. Contact Creditors--close accounts--cut up credit cards--change due dates to 15th of month--monitor statements monthly
5. Stay in contact with Springboard if you receive notices of declined proposals from any creditors -- 1-888-669-2227
6. Start Debt Management Plan by making sure at least $205 is in checking account on 10/2/02 and the 1st of every month
7. Read "Credit When Credit Is Due" and complete financial literacy curriculum
8. Refer others who are struggling with credit card bills, mortgage or rent payments, loans, etc. to 1-800-WISE-PLAN

Action(s) Taken:

☑ Assessed Problems and Solutions   ☑ Budget Development   ☑ Developed Action Steps

Recommendations:

☐ Advised to Handle Finaces (on own)   ☑ Educational Classes

☑ Debt Management Plan   ☐ Housing Assistance

☐ Referred for Legal Advice   ☐ Other _____

☐ Referred Client to Outside Resource   ☐ Other _____

_____   9/5/2002
Client Signature   Date

_____   1st Scheduled Deposit Date: 10/2/2002
Counselor Signature   (MM/DD/YY)

For questions about our services or your debt management plan please call our Client Service Group at 909.781.0114 or toll free at 888.669.2227.

To learn more about how the DMP works and other important information please access our website: www.credit.org.

this book to come up with your own action plan. Find the entries that address your situation, and use our advice to chart a course to financial freedom.

Here are some actions that we recommend for every client:

- *Education.* Whatever the outcome of the counseling, every client is advised to attend our educational seminars and complete the "Credit When Credit Is Due" financial literacy program. This is a requirement, not a recommendation. We recognize that education is the best way to ensure long-term financial success. Fully understanding your financial situation is never a bad thing.
- *Budget.* Part of the education process is attending our budgeting seminars and creating a budget that works for you. There's only so much our counselors can teach in a 90-minute counseling session. Our clients are advised to attend our seminars in order to create a truly effective budget, and we advise you not to skip Chapter 2 if you want to truly master your financial destiny.

Beyond that, you'll have to determine what your action steps need to be if you want to knock out your debt. Just remember to never lose sight of your goals, and you'll always be on the right track.

ANOTHER WAY

There is no one and only way to do anything. It seems that the minute we latch on to any generalization, that generalization is proven wrong the next minute. Just when we decide that defense wins championships, the St. Louis Rams pass their way to Super Bowl. Just when it seems a natural law that low-carbohydrate diets are the shining path to weight loss, somebody loses a hundred pounds eating at Subway, and when we finally became convinced that white men couldn't dance, Michael Jackson turned white.

Exception is the rule, and advice on getting out of debt is no exception. The methods used by Springboard and other counseling agencies and the usual outline in other debt-handling books are tried and true. They can certainly point to many successes, but debt problems are as individual as fingerprints. Yours didn't happen in the same way everyone else's did, and your solutions won't necessarily be the same, either.

This section is designed to offer alternatives to the more general strategies outlined in this chapter. The hope is that you will pick and choose: Add a little of this, snip a little of that, and create a debt plan that fits best with the way you think about money and the way you organize your financial life. We hope to offer techniques that have worked for some people but are often overlooked by most of the available debt literature. Remember that a suggested method is never a rule; it's just a proven suggestion.

That doesn't mean that there can't be any rules.

With that in mind, it will help if you'll accept three rules up front. These are the only absolutes we're giving you.

> *Absolute Rule 1:* You can do it. There is a way out.
>
> *Absolute Rule 2:* Your debt goals and dreams will become reality much sooner if you put some hard work into them. In fact, any goal or dream will be helped by hard work.
>
> *Absolute Rule 3:* You can do the hard work. Even when you think you can't, you really can. Even when you blew it yesterday, you can do it today. There is a way out.

ANOTHER WAY TO THINK ABOUT GOALS

While the type of long-term, specific, measurable goals discussed in this chapter work for most people, there is another way. Some people find themselves discouraged by the mountain they have committed themselves to climb, others weight themselves down with skepticism, and many others are lulled to sleep or despair by their slow progress. For those who have trouble with traditional goals, here are a few alternative goal strategies that have worked for some.

Remember, nothing will work for everybody, and this list of course does not include every possibility. All that's certain is that *something* will work for you if you just work to find it.

1. *Competition.* Educators learn early that for some students, goals in themselves aren't attractive, but beating someone else is. Some people just can't run fast unless there is someone to run

against. If you've identified that type of pride in yourself, there are ways to harness it to solve your debt problem.

Some people have ready competitors right in their households—spouses and roommates, for example. People who can't get behind a goal like "I'll have an emergency fund of $500 and pay off $100 of principal by October" can often get behind something like "I'm going to pay off more debt than my husband this month" or "I'm going to contribute more to the emergency fund this week than my wife."

This kind of thing works even if the other person isn't competing. It makes the goal more immediate and thus more motivational. It also provides feelings of accomplishment more quickly.

Even if you don't have a competitor on hand, you may have experienced the intensity of a 2-hour minesweeper session played just for the glory of beating your own high score. A lot of people find that "I paid off 28 bucks last month; I'm going to do whatever it takes to pay off 29 this month," has the same sort of addictive quality once offered by Pac-Man.

Other competitive people have found that the opponents that goaded them on most were the creditors themselves. "Citibank can't get the best of me!" If this helps you stay committed enough to make the sacrifices and do the hard work, that's great. Use your pride to show them what you've got. Just be sure you don't sound adversarial when you're talking to your creditors on the phone.

What's best about the competition goal approach is that, if nothing else, it helps people get off the floor faster and get back on their plan when they blow it. Competitors know that you can't worry about the last play; you just have to go out and make the next one. If you just stay in the game long enough, something good might happen.

2. *Cooperation.* Cooperation can be just as strong a goal strategy as competition for the right person. Obviously, having families, couples, or friends help each other toward debt goals is important. Consumer Credit Counseling Service or Debtors Anonymous can help if you're feeling that you have less imme-

diate support. But cooperation can be more than just the best way to achieve goals for a family; cooperation can be part of the goals themselves.

You can divide a goal like "$300 worth of principal paid and enough money for a small vacation by July" into even smaller cooperation-based goals, such as

"We'll clip coupons together once a week."

"We'll get up early enough to share a car ride twice a week."

"We'll clean out a closet together every weekend and find something to sell."

"We'll search for a cheaper apartment together."

"We'll make all our Christmas presents together this year."

"We'll pick out movies from the library instead of going out."

There are plenty of possibilities, depending on how bad the situation is. The point of this is that the cooperation gives the goals weight and makes them shared in action, not just in burden. Eventually, some people have found that working and being together becomes the important part or that the mutual activity makes things easier.

3. *Attempts goals.* An attempts goal is a strategy that is used effectively by artists and salespeople. The idea is that instead of focusing on your target, which may be out of your control, you focus on your attempt, which is within your control. For instance, a door-to-door salesperson would change the goal from "sell 10 vacuum cleaners today" to "knock on 150 doors today and show this vacuum cleaner to 20 people."

Sometimes, no matter how good the salesperson is, he or she may not sell 10 machines. But the salesperson can still make the goal, know that he or she went all out, and still have a sense of accomplishment. Plus, the law of averages says that if the pitch is solid, showing the vacuum cleaner to 20 people a day will work out to selling 10. Some days it will be more, some days less, but the salesperson steadily maintains the goal.

When actors change their goal from "getting a big part this year" to "getting a hundred auditions this year," they start getting parts. Even in sports, smart coaches never come into a game saying, "We're going to run for 150 yards today." They can't control that. They say, "We're going to run it 25 times today," and more often than not, that yields the running yards they wanted.

Debt goals can be adapted to this formula as well, especially if you use day-by-day budgeting (see the end of Chapter 2). The emphasis changes from "I'll pay off this much debt" to something like "I'll go without air conditioning one day a week this June" or "I'll take my lunch every day and eat this many ketchup sandwich dinners." Whatever you can handle.

The idea is that you focus on the things that get you there, the journey, instead of the destination. People who have success with this find that paying off 30 grand in medical bills seems impossible, but a goal like having 40 extra bucks by the end of the month seems easy.

Focusing on the details is habit-forming too and trains the mind to find more. People can't convince themselves that using a third of the recommended amount of laundry detergent matters against a 10-grand credit card mountain, but it does matter against a $20 weekly goal. Attempts goals teach you to sweat the small stuff.

4. *A material attachment.* It helps many people to attach some definite reward to their long-term goals. Instead of stopping with "being debt-free on April 15, 2008," add something like "and a brand new kitchen, paid in cash, a year later" or "a week in Hawaii" or whatever floats your boat. The point is that when you visualize, don't just visualize the zeros on your balance statement and the increase in your credit score, and don't visualize some abstract concept like "out from under the heel of 'the man.'" Take it to a specific place, something you could do or have if you were really out of your credit problem.

5. *Winning records.* The only negative aspect of goal setting is that sometimes things will happen and you won't make it. It's important to remember that all you have to do is win more than you lose. The car broke down and you didn't make your goal. Suck it up, staunch the bleeding; you still had 3 good months to 1 bad. This was never going to happen overnight.

Winning records come from analysis. The VCR revolutionized sports, dance, drama, public speaking, comedy—the list is endless. The reason for this is that participants could analyze their performance after the fact, think over what went wrong, and plan a way to improve. When you blow a month or a week or a day, figure out how and why. A lot of "bad luck" can be avoided if you're honest and know what situations to avoid.

6. *A quick goal myth.* Most authorities, when discussing goals, will include the advice "make them flexible." That's not necessarily a good idea. To be most effective, real objectives have to be firm. Don't allow room for compromise. The problem with "something to fall back on" is that people fall back on it. It's better to have a solid goal and fail by a smidgen than to get in the habit of letting yourself off the hook.

A FINAL WORD ABOUT GOALS

Mix and match, cut and add, find something that works best for you, but find something and commit to it. Remember, the only rule is that you can do it.

Chapter 2

Budgeting

We've heard others say that budgets are like diets: They never work, and in the end they leave you worse off than you were when you started.

We flatly disagree.

Budgets do work, especially in crisis situations, and even if you go off of your budget, you've still gotten through a rough time because of it. Sure, dieters often regain the weight they lost after a diet ends, and maybe some consumers end up spending the money they saved while they were on a budget.

So what? It's *your* money! Spend it all you want. Like Ben Franklin said, "A penny saved is a penny earned," and if you saved money by smart budgeting, you earned it. The true worst-case scenario here is if you quit your budget and rack up a mountain of new *debt*. We're going to make sure that doesn't happen.

Of course, we don't recommend that you blow all the money you'll save if you budget intelligently, but the main reason we want you to go on a budget is to avoid incurring new debt. The extra money you'll save is a nice bonus.

There are three things you need to know before you construct a budget.

To construct a budget, you'll need to know your expenses, income, and goals. Your expenses are the hardest to get a handle on, and the most important.

We regularly offer budgeting seminars at Springboard headquarters in Riverside, California. They're free and open to the public, and people are welcome to come back repeatedly. Many do, choosing to attend every few months for a refresher course in budgeting, or to get renewed inspiration, or just to ask a few questions.

Sometimes, a person will come back a few months later and this conversation will take place:

Client: "I tried that budgeting stuff. It didn't work."
Us: "Did you use the techniques we talked about?"
Client: "I did everything! Nothing worked."
Us. "Everything? Did you track your expenses for a full month?"
Client: "Well, no. . . ."

It happens every time. The number-one reason that budgets fail, we're convinced, is because people do not fully track their expenses before embarking on a budget.

There is no way to succeed in budgeting if you don't know what your current spending looks like. If you're going to make positive changes in your personal money management, you have to know what mistakes you're making now.

So what you need to do is spend a month tracking all of your spending. How? Good question.

TRACKING YOUR EXPENSES

It's important that you track your expenses for at least a full month, track them every day, and track everything. That means that if you put 50 cents in a vending machine, you need to track it.

You need to track every penny, but you don't necessarily need to track every item you purchase. For example, if you spend $50 at the grocery store, just track it as "groceries." Don't worry about each thing you bought.

Every consumer is different, and so we can't provide one catchall method for tracking expenses that will work for all of you. Here are a few suggestions. Pick the one that fits you best.

- *Software.* Jeff uses software to track his expenses. This is a good solution because most of us have some kind of money management software that came with our personal computer that we've probably never used. Use it! There are a lot of good software packages out there that will help you manage your personal finances and provide lots of extra tools to help you create a budget that accurately reflects your spending habits.
- *Day planner.* If you carry a day planner or calendar, consider tracking your expenses there. All you have to do is jot down what you spend each day on that day's calendar entry. It's important to track day by day so that you know what you're spending during different times of the month, and using a calendar is a great way to do it.
- *Receipts.* One method that's initially easy is to keep all your receipts and toss them into a shoebox or into envelopes, then do all of the tallying later. Just make sure they're separated by date so that you can map your spending over the course of the month. And if you buy something and don't get a receipt (stop buying candy from that vending machine!), you'll need to jot the date and amount (and what you purchased) on a slip of paper to substitute for the missing receipt.
- *Forms.* Thom uses this method; he'll create a chart on graph paper to track where all the money's going and how much he needs in order to get through the rest of the month. (See Figure 2-1 for an example.)
- *Notebook.* The simplest solution may be to just carry a small pocket notebook and jot down what you spend as you spend it.

The act of tracking can be fun, but it's more likely to be tedious. Our experience is that it will get particularly annoying during the second week. You'll get to a point where you'd rather do absolutely anything other than track your day's spending yet again. But stick with it. It will get easier, we promise. Keep tracking, and as the days go by, it will become easier and more routine—just another thing you do every day, like brushing your teeth (please tell us you brush your teeth every day).

Map out your spending over the course of the month (see Figure 2-2). That way you can get an accurate picture of not just where your money is

Figure 2-1 Thom's Budgeting Form

Date	Utilities/ Rent/Bills	Credit Card/ Student Loan	Food	Entertainment	Gas	Necessities
1	375	50			15	
2			25	5		10
3						
4		25	5			
5						
6						
7						
8						
9						
10						
11						
12						
13						
14						
15						
16						
17						
18						
19						
20						
21						
22						
23						
24						
25						
26						
27						
28						
29						
30						
31						
Month End Totals	480	320	105	70	65	25

Miscellaneous	Total Spent	Total Earned	Day +/-	Month +/-
	440	65	-375	-375
	40	65	+25	-350
	0	65	+65	-285
	30	65	+35	-250
30	1150	1225	-	+75

(See the section in Chapter 2, "Another Way to Budget")

Figure 2-2 Map Out Your Spending

Use a form like this one to record all of your expenses each day. Make copies of this page as needed.

Date	Mortgage or Rent	Property Taxes	Insurance (Home- owners)	HOA	Gas/ Electric	Telephone (Cell and Pager)	Water/ Sewer/ Trash	Groceries/ Household	Car Payment
1									
2									
3									
4									
5									
6									
7									
8									
9									
10									
11									
12									
13									
14									
15									
16									
17									
18									
19									
20									
21									
22									
23									
24									
25									
26									
27									
28									
29									
30									
31									
total									

2nd Car Payment	DMV Registration	Auto Insurance	Gas/ Oil	Day Care	Child Support/ Alimony	Taxes	Medical	Cable TV	Savings	Misc.

going, but when it's going. If you tend to spend a lot at the end of the month, you'll want to know that. When you spend is as important as where you spend.

Now that you have a picture of your spending, assess where you stand. Here's where you'll learn things about yourself.

Jeff's story: When Jeff did the tracking for the first time, he expected grocery spending to be his biggest transgression. From his well-worn barbecue grill to his championship chili recipe, Jeff expected to learn that he was spending too much at the supermarket.

He was completely wrong. Grocery spending wasn't the problem— his food budget was well within the national averages. No, Jeff's problem was spending too much at places like Best Buy and Circuit City. He had no idea until he tracked his expenses that he was spending so much on software and DVDs and other things that he didn't need.

That's the kind of lesson the tracking exercise can teach you. If you really get an accurate picture of your spending, you may see that you're not in such bad shape after all. Sometimes a simple fix (stop going to Best Buy!) can work wonders.

NEEDS VS. WANTS: THE TWO TYPES OF EXPENSES

Jeff's problem was the same as most consumers': too much spending on Wants.

Now we all know our English grammar, so we know what Needs (hot water, food, shelter) and Wants (magazines, video games, designer shoes) are. Sometimes, though, we get confused. We spend way too much on Wants, many times even tricking ourselves into thinking that they're really Needs.

But be aware of the difference, and keep reminding yourself of it. When you're trying to cut down on your spending, the Wants are where you're going to make the tough choices.

- *Ignore commercials.* Television commercials (and all advertising, for that matter) are designed to persuade you that you need things that you really just want.

   When Thom sees a commercial for the Ford Thunderbird, he's convinced that he needs that car. What stops him from running out and buying it (aside from its price) is the realization that while he does need a car, he doesn't need that particular car.

Be more sophisticated than advertising; never, ever blindly accept what advertisers try to tell you (see Chapter 8 for more on saying no to salespeople).

- *Not all Needs are alike.* Thom needs a car. Most of us do, in this day and age. But what kind? What if Thom had a wife who was pregnant with twins? Wouldn't a station wagon be more appropriate than a sporty convertible?

  Don't justify overspending by writing it off as a Need. Yes, you need to eat, but you don't need to eat prime rib at a four-star restaurant every night. You probably need telephone service, but do you need caller ID, call forwarding, digital voice mail, and all the other services the phone company would gladly sell you?

- *Is it a Need or a Want? A quick test.* Before you purchase something, simply ask yourself, "How did I get by for so long without this?" The honest answer to that question will tell you if you're really dealing with a Need or if this is a Want that can be put off a bit longer.

BUDGET GUIDELINES

There are certain accepted guidelines for what your overall budget should look like. You may have heard some of them (spend one-third of your income on housing, one-quarter on transportation, and so on).

The spending guidelines that follow are given as ranges rather than hard percentages. Depending on any number of factors, your budget may differ slightly from these norms. One rule is firm, though: You can't have a total of more than 100 percent—you're not the government, and you can't engage in deficit spending.

Also, the percentages below should be based on net income, or take-home pay.

- *Housing—30 to 40 percent.* This includes mortgage or rent, property taxes, insurance, repairs, improvements, and so on. We generally say that a third of your income should be spent on housing, but there are many areas of the United States where this is increasingly impossible. In southern California, housing costs currently tend to account for as much as half of a typical consumer's budget.

- *Utilities—8 to 15 percent.* Include in this category gas, electricity, water, trash, sewer, and any kind of phone service (cellular or land-based). Include pagers or Internet access in this category only if it's a Need and not a Want.
- *Food—10 to 20 percent.* This is self-explanatory, but be sure to include pet food within this area of spending.
- *Auto and transportation—15 to 25 percent.* Contrary to what car salespeople will tell you, your car payment should not be 25 percent of your income (never trust what a car salesperson tells you, ever). This 25 percent represents your total transportation budget. That means that insurance, gas, oil changes and repairs, parking, and public transportation should all be included.
- *Medical—8 to 15 percent.* This includes insurance premiums, prescriptions, doctor's and dentist's bills (and again, veterinarian's bills—if you have pets, you have to include them in the family budget).
- *Clothing—3 to 5 percent.* This includes all clothing purchases, shoes, alterations, cleaning and laundering, and so on.
- *Personal and miscellaneous—5 to 10 percent.* This is a big issue for most consumers. We're 99 percent certain that everyone reading this is over budget in this area. There are so many things to cram into this little 10 percent sliver of your budget—entertainment, hobbies, postage, tobacco (quit smoking), cosmetics, haircuts, cable TV, magazine subscriptions, and so on—that we're convinced that this is why so many Americans struggle with debt. Most of the things in this category are Wants, not Needs, so they should be the first things eliminated when you are trying to cut back on spending.
- *Savings and investment—5 to 10 percent.* This is absolutely crucial, and no one does it. We already discussed the importance of saving an emergency fund in Chapter 1. Unfortunately, most Americans don't do it. They use up this 10 percent on the personal and miscellaneous category. Make contributing to this category the first priority in your new budget. As for investing, we advise you to get your emergency savings fund established before tackling the stock market.

- *Monthly installments—10 to 20 percent.* This includes all credit card payments, personal and student loans, and any other debt payments. Twenty percent is the absolute maximum here. If you spend more than a fifth of your gross income on installment debt, you're headed for disaster. For most consumers, even 20 percent is too high. Try to get this down to 15 percent or less, especially if you are on a fixed income.

CREATING A NEW BUDGET

Now that you've tracked your spending and compared it to the budget guidelines, it's time to propose a new budget that will work for you.

This is where most people will start. They simply skip to this step and prepare a new budget to live by from now on. This is why budgets fail. This is why irresponsible pundits can blithely declare that budgets are like diets: They never work.

But trust us, if you do it the way we've advised—track your spending completely for a full month before you get to this step—your budget will work.

Sketch out a complete picture of what your spending should look like (see Figure 2-3). As you're doing so, refer to last month's spending—that will help you make sure that your new budget is realistic. Anyone can say, "I'm only going to spend $150 on groceries next month." But if you've been spending $450 per month for the last year, then you're proposing the impossible.

Keeping your past spending in mind will help you propose sensible cuts that will allow your budget to work.

BALANCING YOUR BUDGET

This sounds so much easier than it is. Add up all of your spending, subtract it from your income, and make sure that you end up with a positive number. If you don't have enough income to cover all of your budgeted spending, then you'll have to revisit your budget.

The first thing to look at in this situation is your goals. Don't tamper with the emergency savings fund goal—this is a must.

Figure 2-3 Monthly Budget

Necessary Expenses	Current Spending	Proposed Spending
Housing, Rent/Mortgage		
2nd Mortgage		
Property Taxes		
Insurance		
HOA Dues		
Gas/Electricity		
Water/Sewer/Garbage		
Telephone		
Food		
Groceries		
Dining Out		
At Work/At School		
Insurance		
Health/Dental/Vision		
Life		
Disability		
Medical Care		
Doctor/Chiropractor		
Optometrist/Lenses		
Dental/Orthodontist		
Prescriptions/Medications		
Counseling/Therapy		
Transportation		

Discretionary Expenses	Current Spending	Proposed Spending
Personal		
Beauty/Barber		
Clothing/Jewelry		
Cosmetics		
Manicure/Other		
Entertainment		
Cable TV		
Movie/Video		
Dining Out		
Sports/Hobbies/Clubs		
Vacations/Travel		
Books/Magazines		
CDs/Tapes		
Internet Access		
Miscellaneous		
Pet Care/Veterinary		
Gifts		
Pager/Cell Phone		
Postage		
Cigarettes/Alcohol		
Donations/Tithing		
Other		
Other		
Total Discretionary Expenses:		

Installment Debt Payments

Creditor Name	Monthly Payments
Total Debt Payments:	

Car Payment 1	
Car Payment 2	
Insurance (Auto)	
Gas/Oil	
Repairs	
DMV	
Tolls/Parking	
Public Transportation/Taxi	
Child Care	
Daycare/Sitting	
Child Support/Alimony	
Miscellaneous	
Banking Fees	
Laundry	
Union Dues	
Other	
Other	
Income Taxes	
Prior Year	
Estimated Tax Payments (Self-Employed)	
Savings	
Emergency	
Goals	
Total Essential Expenses:	

But if your budget isn't balancing, consider extending your deadline for your other goals. The longer you save toward a particular goal, the less you need to save from every paycheck, giving you more to work with.

The second thing to look at is discretionary spending. That's right, the Wants. Something will have to go. Maybe you'll have to downgrade to basic cable, or dispense with it entirely. Maybe you really should quit smoking after all. Whatever you do, make sure you examine your discretionary spending before you do anything more drastic.

SAVINGS STRATEGIES TO MAKE YOUR BUDGET WORK

The point of all this budgeting is to stop incurring new debt and to set aside money for the things you really want and need. It will work—maybe too well. When some consumers budget and free up extra money, they feel too great a temptation to spend it.

You want to save the extra money you're setting aside when you budget—for your emergency savings fund, for one thing, and to reach your financial goals, for another. And if you have money left over after that, well, you're certainly free to spend it. It's your money, after all. But make those spending decisions intelligently—save that money until you know you've got something important to spend it on.

When Jeff saved up some extra money after 6 months of budgeting, he felt flush enough to return to Circuit City and indulge himself. An Xbox, a few games, and no guilt—because he paid cash and didn't use a credit card. He was just rewarding himself for all of his successful budgeting. His emergency fund was still intact, his budget was working fine, no worries. That's why we budget, right? To be able to go out and buy those things we want without having to incur new debt.

Except that a coworker managed to get tickets to game seven of the World Series a week later. And Jeff got to watch it in a sports bar instead of from the stands, because he'd blown his discretionary fund on consumer electronics.

So think about how you can save all that extra money you're going to have without running out and spending it indiscriminately. Here are some suggestions.

- *Direct deposit.* Your bank account will always be the best place to save your money. If you really want to hide it under the mattress, by all means do so—but don't come crying to us when the house burns down or you get burglarized.

  Most direct deposit arrangements will allow you to divide the funds between different accounts. So if you're having your paycheck automatically deposited to your bank account, you can have a specified amount or percentage sent to savings and the rest deposited into checking. Some systems can even send money to different financial institutions altogether, and it's certainly easier to save money that you never see in the first place.

- *Convenience.* Perhaps it would be smart to find a bank or credit union that's a bit less convenient. Sure, it's nice to have an ATM from your bank on every corner, but this may make it far too easy for you to get to your money and spend it. Consider putting your savings in an out-of-the-way financial institution. Force yourself to work a little harder to get at that money before you spend it.

- *The envelope method.* This famous method is taught far and wide by credit counseling agencies everywhere (including Springboard), but frankly, it makes us nervous.

  In the envelope method, you create envelopes for the different items on your budget, and mark each of them accordingly. So you'd have an envelope marked "Rent—$500," another marked "Phone bill—$75," and so on. Then you simply put cash in the envelopes as you get it until you build up the required amount.

  This method can help in a crisis or in certain circumstances. For example, Thom used this method when he was working as a waiter, was bringing home a lot of cash tips, and had an inconsistent income.

  However, this involves keeping a lot of cash on hand, and theft or disaster could occur at any time. If you do use the envelope method to save money, be careful—consider getting a fireproof safe.

- *Save change.* One way to set aside extra money is to use only paper money and save all of your change. If the tab comes to $5.41, give them $6 and keep the 59¢—even if you have the change on hand. Then throw all the loose change in a piggy bank or jar. You can save a surprising amount of money by doing this.

SIX BUDGET LEAKS AND HOW TO PLUG THEM

One of the reasons we want you to keep tracking your spending after you begin to live on a budget is so that you can spot leaks and plug them.

You'll have them: small trickles of money that seep out of your budget and threaten to wreck everything.

1. *Food.* First, if you end up spending more on food than you budgeted for, it's probably because you dine out too often. It's five times more expensive to dine out than it is to prepare meals for yourself. So your first order of business when plugging this leak is to cut back on going out to eat.

    Some people like to dine out, though. It's their form of entertainment; it's more important to them than buying new clothes, running the air conditioner, or feeding the dog. Well, if you're one of these people, and you really want to keep dining out, then you have to budget for it. Make dining out a short-term goal every month, and set aside extra money specifically for that. And when that money's spent, you're done. Sorry, but you can't go out to eat until next month.

    As for the other big chunk of your food budget, groceries, there are some strategies that can help you save:
    - *Shop with a list.* This is an age-old bit of advice. Just remember to stick to your list; it does you no good if you just use it as a rough guide. Jeff has been known to take a pen to the store and add items to his list when shopping. This, obviously, completely defeats the purpose.
    - *Don't shop hungry.* This is another old chestnut that happens to be true. Go to the grocery store on an empty stomach, and you'll end up buying way more than you need.

- *Shop alone.* The more people you take with you to the grocery store (kids, spouse, and so on), the more things will end up in your cart that you didn't put there. Go by yourself and maintain control of your grocery shopping.
- *Coupons.* Be careful when using them. They can save you money, but often they're just advertising tools that are designed to get you to buy expensive name-brand items that you wouldn't normally buy and may not need. Make sure you're really saving money when you use coupons—find a grocery store in your area that doubles coupons if you want to use them.
- *Know how grocers work.* The margins in the grocery business are razor thin, so grocers have to be really good at what they do—convincing you to spend more. They'll put the most expensive stuff at eye level, and the more affordable items will be down by the floor or up on a higher shelf. Look around to get the best deal.

  Realize that grocers will move items regularly to keep you looking. Think your favorite cereal is on aisle 6? Not this week—they've moved it, and now you'll have to search for it. And while you do, you'll get to see all of the other great bargains they've laid out for you. It's a trap! And this brings us to our next point.
- *Stay out of the aisles.* Think about the layout of your favorite grocery store. Chances are that everything you need on a regular basis—dairy, produce, bread, meats—is on the outside perimeter of the store. So think of that when planning your shopping. For your regular weekly shopping trips, stay out of the aisles (that's where they'll get you to buy more than you need) and just make a quick run around the outside of the store, getting those staples that you need regularly. Then, once a month or so, make a big shopping trip where you can scour the aisles for the flour, sugar, canned goods, paper products, and so on—all that stuff that you can stock up on.

2. *Retail shopping.* Just as with groceries, shop with a list. Make a list of what you need from Wal-Mart or Kmart or Target or wherever:

tube socks, laundry detergent, motor oil. It doesn't matter that it isn't edible. The important thing is that you plan your spending.

The number-one form of overspending isn't buying too much, or even buying what you don't need. Most people overspend by paying too much for things. So comparison-shop—it's easier than ever with the Internet at our fingertips. Whatever you're looking at on the store shelf, chances are that someone somewhere else is selling it for less. Find them, and buy it there instead.

And one final thing: If shopping is a form of entertainment for you, find a cheaper hobby. There's nothing wrong with window-shopping, but if spending money is your idea of a good time, you're going to have trouble conquering your debt.

Turn to Chapter 8 for more advice on shopping smart.

3. *Entertainment.* People often spend more than they plan to on entertainment because of the impulsive nature of it. It's unlikely that you can predict every time the gang from work will invite you out for an evening of fun, so it's hard to have the money set aside. But that's what you have to do.

Think of creating a discretionary entertainment fund. Set aside money for entertainment without a specific plan for every dollar. The idea is to have enough to handle whatever unpredictable entertainment expense should pop up. Of course, you have to have some discipline, and when the fund for this month is spent, it's spent—you'll have to tell the gang at work that you can't join them this time. Maybe next month.

Another thing to consider is free entertainment. Read your local paper, and look for free concerts and events. You may be surprised how often these kinds of events are offered.

Finally, there are the movies. They're the number-one entertainment outlet for Americans, and we spend a bundle on them. You can spend less on the cinema, though:

- *Plan ahead.* If you like the movies, make sure you set aside money in your budget to attend them. Don't let a trip to the movie theatre be an impulsive spending spree.
- *Beware of the snack bar.* Just as when you go to the grocery store, don't go to the movies on an empty stomach. Theatre

owners make most of their money selling you sodas and pop-corn, not selling you movie tickets. Not that this is a big rev-elation: Items at the snack bar are famously overpriced, and if you've ever been to the movies, you already know it.

- *Discounts.* See matinee shows, use coupons where you can, and keep that old student ID. Jeff's been getting the student discount for 10 years with his.
- *Find a reviewer you trust.* Don't gamble your hard-earned money going to a movie that might stink. Find a reviewer that you tend to agree with to help steer you away from the turkeys. Ask your friends and family as well.

4. *Kids.* There's no telling what kids are going to cost you in a giv-en month. But if you've got them, they're going to complicate your attempt to live on a budget. See Chapter 10 of this book for a thorough discussion of this challenge.

5. *Auto repairs, veterinarian's bills, emergency medical expens-es.* These expenses aren't really leaks. Attendees at our bud-geting seminars regularly bring them up, but a leak, to us, is that slow trickle of money out of the budget that wasn't planned for. Emergency expenses, by definition, can't be planned for. To deal with this category, it's crucial that you're building up your emergency savings fund. If your car breaks down unexpectedly and you need it to get to work and earn more money, then you can use your emergency fund to get it fixed. Building up ample savings is the best way to handle these situations when they occur.

6. *ATM.* If the other things in this list are leaks, then the ATM card is the faucet. This is the thing from which all the money flows. Think about it; you can't overspend if you don't have the cash.

Our advice is to leave the ATM card at home as often as possible. That goes double for debit cards—a great convenience, but potentially a costly one.

Say you're at the grocery store, and you've budgeted to spend $100 on this shopping trip. If the total bill is $107, and you've got that debit card, you'll probably pay the $7 extra. Now your budget has sprung a leak. But if you take only a $100 bill into the grocery store, you can't possibly spend that extra $7. You'll have to take something back (this is the one time it's okay to take your kids to the grocery store—in case you need a scapegoat). Now, $7 might not seem like much, but it adds up, and small leaks become big ones.

ANOTHER WAY TO BUDGET

As we said at the end of Chapter 1, there's always another way to do things. Budgeting in particular is a widely varied science—there are lots of ways to do it that will work. The trick is finding the way that works *for you*.

Budgeting is often the most painful part of getting credit back on track, and, worse, it's the place where the giving up begins in most of the people who give up.

"I tried and tried, but I could never stick to my budget. The failure built up until I felt like I just wouldn't make it." The best alternative form of budgeting for people who feel that way is day-by-day budgeting.

Day-by-day budgeting makes things easier by eliminating budget categories, so that there is less focus on what goes where and more on how much, which is the real question.

You still have to figure out what you are spending, especially on bills, but you can break it down in a way that makes everything more flexible and approachable. Here is a demonstration.

You find out exactly how much you're bringing home each month. Remember, that's not how much you make, it's take-home pay—what's on your check. For most people it's fairly fixed, although waiters and commissioned salespeople may have to average. (If you're one of these people, it's actually easier, because you have a little more control over what you can make. Just set a minimum and work with that figure.) Let's use an actual case. We'll call him Mel.

Mel brings home $1300 a month. Here are his bills:

He pays $485 in rent.
$60 for electric
$30 for phone (always estimate high on anything that fluctuates)
$40 for car insurance
$35 for health insurance

$35 for cable
$20 for Internet access

Debt load

$98 is his student loan payment.
$87 was his last minimum on Citibank. Plan for $90.
$76 was his last minimum on Providian. Plan for $80.
$39 on a medical bill.

So, his expenses total $1005 per month.

To start his day-by-day budget, he has to find a few averages. His $1300 in income divided by a 30-day month gives him $43.33 a day; call it $43. His $1005 in bills divided by 30 comes to $33.50; call it $34. Basically, Mel has 9 bucks a day to get him through gas and food and entertainment. Don't think of it as "$295; where should it go?" Think of it as 9 bucks. That's it.

Mel's goals include zero days. He wants to have four zero days a week—days when he spends nothing. Every time he gets a zero day, he's just added 9 bucks to what he can spend.

Every single day he figures out where he is. "I spent 15 on gas yesterday, so I was 6 bucks down. But I made 9 today, so I'm 3 bucks up. If I eat something old in the cupboard, I can be up 12 tomorrow."

Day-by-day budgeters constantly watch how much they are up or down. They never have to worry about "Can I go to karaoke tonight? How much is in my entertainment budget?" They don't know, and they don't care. All they know is that they are only 8 bucks up. If they want to make their goals, they can spend only 7.

Having it on your mind like that keeps you focused and maintains a sense of urgency. You want the triple fat burger, but if you're only $3.50 up, it will have to be fries and water. Day-by-dayers never guess. They never say things like, "I think I'll be all right." They aren't surprised at the huge amount they spent on groceries, and they don't even care, because all they know is that on the last day of the month, they were 11 up. It's a win. They train themselves to divorce whatever savings they are putting away from reality. That money does not exist; all they have today is 9 bucks. If they want a new CD, they'd better pull some zero days.

Even families can get into the accumulation of zero days: stars on the calendar for each one, ten stars is a walk to Dairy Queen, and so on.

What Mel found, and most people will find it with him, is that saving money gets to be a little obsessive. "The electric bill was a little lower this month and I saved on phone calls." "I thought I was 11 up, but I was really 27." The other nice thing is, the minimums he started with have gone down after a few months, and he's paying more on principal. When he looks at the bill 6 months later, he's got a minimum of $69 instead of $76. In a tight month—December because of Christmas, or evil February*—he can just pay the minimums to free up an extra $20, or maybe more. *(As a rule, though, don't pay the minimums for more than 3 consecutive months.)*

If traditional budgets are giving you fits or bringing you down, you can try day-by-day budgeting for a while. If it becomes clear that this is not going to work for you, try something else or some kind of mix. As always, there's no one way, just a way.

---

*If you aren't on salary, then you worked fewer days and made less money in February, but the rent stayed the same. Valentine's Day took a chunk out of you, and in most of America the February heating bills are the highest because it's still cold, but heating oil is getting short. The length of winter makes it easier to get depressed, too. Watch out for February.

Chapter 3

Basic Debt Handling

WHY DEBT CAN BE A GOOD THING

If you were to walk into Springboard Non-Profit Consumer Credit Management's headquarters office, you'd see lots of cut-up credit cards—melted into artwork that adorns the walls, in clear plastic bottles in our counselors' offices, in a fishbowl in the CEO's office. We'd wager that most of the other agencies in the Consumer Credit Counseling Service network have the same collection of mutilated plastic.

Seeing those things might give you the impression that we're anti-credit, that we don't think you should have credit cards.

That's not true. We're pro-credit, in a big way. We think that credit's good, and that everyone should have it, use it, and participate fully in America's great economy.

It's not the use of credit we preach against. It's the *mis*use of credit that has to stop.

Why? So that you can build a good credit rating.

Why build credit? To preserve your access to debt.

Debt allows you to get a college education, buy a house, buy a car, or start a business. All of these things are great reasons to get into debt. But if you don't have good credit, good luck finding someone to lend you that money.

So remember, this journey isn't about swearing off debt forever; it's about restoring your credit and maintaining your access to that good debt that can help you live the life you deserve.

DIAGNOSIS: AM I IN TROUBLE?

Warning signs are everywhere. Each book, article, and brochure has the obligatory "10 signs of debt trouble" section; but really, if you bought this book and you're worried about being in debt trouble, then you probably are. If you've missed a payment and can't make it up, or if it would be easy to find yourself in that situation, then you definitely are in trouble. It's that simple.

There are, however, a few diagnostic tools that counseling agencies use that are much more scientific than the old 10-question quiz. Because of the individual nature of debt problems, none of them tell you exactly where you are, but they can at least give you a quantified picture of your situation. Sometimes, you just need some hard numbers.

Debt Load and Debt-to-Income Ratios

One of the number systems that yields some useful information is debt load.

When you figure your debt load, you are basically just trying to find out how much of your paycheck isn't yours at all or what percentage of your income is already spoken for.

First, you must figure up all of your debt payments. This is everything on which you pay interest, except perhaps your house payment. Say the total is $500. Then you must figure your net income. If you've already done some budgeting research, this will be easy. If not, please go back and do some. Some counselors will go by gross, but our recommendation is to always work with what you really have, so use only what you actually bring home.

Now you just figure what you are paying out as a percentage of what you are bringing in. For example, $500 in debt payments divided by $1500 in income puts you at 33 percent. Now you have a hard number, so what does that mean?

It depends on whom you ask, but most counselors agree that you should never get over 20 percent, and that if you are over 20 percent, you should get some help now.

Progress Percentage

Another percentage that you can look at is your progress percentage. Progress percentage is a little harder to determine because credit cards are specifically designed to cut down your progress. Minimums are low so that you will stay in debt forever, and nowhere on your statement will it tell you just how much progress you are making. That's okay; they can't keep you down. You can figure it out.

First, add up all of your principals. You probably already did. Let's say you have $10,000 in student loans, $5000 in credit cards, $6000 still owed on your car, $2000 for a legal fee, and $60,000 on your house. That's 83 grand in debt.

Start with your credit cards, because they will carry the worst interest. The statement should show your previous balance. Subtract your new balance from that. That sad figure shows you how much principal you actually paid off last month. Say it's $50. Now divide that by the principal, in this case 5000 bucks. Multiply the answer by 100 to get your percentage. In this case, that's 1 percent. That's how much progress you made on your credit card debt—1 percent.

You can figure how much principal you paid on everything with a little work. Let's say you paid off $210 of principal on your $83,000 debt. You made 0.25 percent progress. *Point* 25. Not too pretty.

While you're figuring your progress percentage, figure it for each individual debt. This will help you see where you may need to shift money or put the most extra cash. If you are making only 1 percent progress on your credit card but 5 percent on your car loan, is there a way to even things out, to shift money to higher-interest, lower-progress debts?

Some people will tell you to figure your progress again without the house payment. They will say that if you are paying on a house, your progress is a little better than it looks because the principal you are paying off is becoming equity. That's true, but your point is to make progress against interest, and no matter how much of that house payment is coming back to you, a good deal of it is still going to the lender.

Okay, so now you can see how much progress you are making, assuming you aren't racking up more debt each month. But it's still a percentage; it's just as relative as the others. Is it enough? How do you know? Well, if you aren't making any progress, you know you're in trouble.

TIME IS MONEY? MONEY IS TIME

If you are making 1 percent progress on your debt, then you've got 8 years and 4 months before it's paid off. If, still using the last example, you have $83,000 and you're making 0.25 percent progress on your debt, you've got a little over 33 years before it's paid off. That is, of course, assuming that you never borrow another dollar—put something on a credit card, borrow from a friend, or borrow from some other source—and that for 400 months you are always able to make these payments. The bonus, at least on the credit cards, is that your progress is increasing with every payment, and so you will be able to shave some time off of those 400 months. Most other loans are spread out evenly over time.

The point is, 33 years and 8 years are real quantities that you can imagine. Do you want to still be paying these debts in 33 years? Will you want to be in the same house? Will you want to make improvements to it? Will your car last that long? Will you have kids starting college in that time? Is the amount you are paying on your debt allowing you to save for retirement and handle emergencies? How good is your health plan? How safe is your job? The answers to these questions can now be weighed against a number of years, not a nebulous percentage.

Just take the amount you pay in principal, whatever it is; realistically, it's more complex than 1 percent. Let's say it's something odd like 0.561 percent, so that on $83,000 you are paying $465 in principal each month. Now just divide the principal, $83,000, by the amount you're knocking off of it each month, $465. What you get is the number of months; in this example, it's rounded up to 179 months. Divide that by 12 and you have the number of years; in this example, it's about 15.

Fifteen years. That's something you can get your mind around. If the number of years looks like too many to you, too risky considering the other things you might like to buy or other things you might need, you know you've got to make some changes. And the best thing about finding this number is that if or when you decide to look for credit counseling or a debt management plan, you can weigh this against the number of years it promises you. Is the plan really cutting any time off here? If so, is the amount significant? Is your progress percentage really going to go up? Now you'll know.

HOW DID I GET HERE?

So you answered questions in a quiz, you figured out some ratio, your card got declined at the drugstore, or you walked out to your driveway and found that your car had been repossessed. One way or another, you've figured out that you need some help. So first things first; if you're getting out, you need to know how you got in. How *did* you get here?

Two ways spring to mind.

You Spent Money You Didn't Have

The most common way this happens is simply not earning enough. We already discussed the difference between Needs and Wants, but what if you are truly buying only Needs and still falling behind? Then you've just got to make more money. That is, of course, a lot easier said than done.

Another way this happens is that you shop impulsively or compulsively or just that your standard of living is more lavish than you think. Impulsive spending is when you just see something and suddenly want it. This was not an item you planned for, nor was it something you budgeted for or saw on a day when you were $30 ahead of schedule. This was something you just saw and thought, "Wow, I (or my boyfriend or my kid or my sister) would really like that."

One thing that eludes a lot of shoppers, especially people who have new nieces or nephews or babies of any sort in the family, is the gift impulse. They come in saying, "But I truly don't have stupid stuff in my house. Not a 'Seal-a-Meal' in sight." But a close look at the credit card statement reveals a new Sit-n-Spin for cousin Joey.

Impulsive spending is insidious in that by its nature it sneaks up on people and preys on their emotions. "I'm just sick of all my clothes." "She dumped me. I need something to make me feel better. How about a PlayStation?" Or the very worst, and please be on your guard and be strong: "I'm never going to get out of debt: I might as well charge a plasma screen TV."

Compulsive shoppers have a different problem. They can't stop. They leave to pick up their dry cleaning and end up deep inside the mall staring at a pearl-handled lint brush. Their reasons for shopping aren't the same as impulsive spending. Compulsive shoppers buy things they don't even need; for them the act of shopping is an attempt to reduce anxiety or depression, or perhaps to ease a perceived deprivation.

Here are 10 signs of compulsive shopping:

1. Shopping to relieve anger or depression
2. Spending that disrupts normal life
3. Conflict with loved ones over shopping
4. Lying to family and friends about shopping
5. Feelings of elation when shopping
6. Frequently taking cash from others and putting their purchases on one's card
7. Shopping feels like doing something forbidden
8. Guilt or shame after shopping
9. Purchases that are never unwrapped or used
10. Purchasing things on credit for which one wouldn't spend cash

If you have experienced several of these symptoms, you may need help from a professional therapist. Some sort of 12-step group (like Debtors Anonymous) might help, too. Compulsive shopping is not to be taken lightly; even reducing your debt and rebuilding good credit can be a problem, since it frees you up to spend more. Compulsive shoppers need psychological help.

You Gambled

You gambled on (your education, your health, your job security, your spouse, your kid, your talent, an investment, or a horse) and you lost.

The fact is, most people with a debt crisis are victims of things they just didn't count on. No one expects to lose his or her job or contract rickets or get a costly divorce. People are thrilled when their children are accepted to Brown, but their bankbooks are not. And there are always the artists or entrepreneurs who give up their steady incomes to pursue a dream and end up in trouble. Even more common are the teachers, lawyers, or social workers who, after years of college and hefty student loans, realize that this is not the career for them.

NOW WHAT?

Not only are debt problems of this nature usually more pressing than simple bad spending, they're also less predictable and tougher to fix. Tougher, but not even close to impossible. With millions of dollars of debt, a major bankruptcy, and a divorce, Donald Trump became a millionaire again in 3 years. Your $80,000 deficit seems like the inevitable end of the world, but it isn't. Yes, you'll have to grit your teeth for a while, but you'll use them to smile again soon enough. You can do this. Let's get started.

There are several ways to go about knocking out your debts. To some degree or another, it's going to involve paying them off, unless your situation is totally hopeless. How you pay them off, however, is something over which you have some control.

Refinancing

Mortgage refinancing loans are more popular than ever, mainly because of favorable interest rates. The two primary reasons people refinance their mortgage loans are

1. To take advantage of lower interest rates
2. To convert some of the equity in their homes into cash

There are other reasons to refinance, of course. Converting from an adjustable-rate mortgage (ARM) to a fixed-rate mortgage might be a good reason. But for our purposes, let's focus on the two reasons just given.

Each situation is different, so you'll have to calculate for yourself whether it's worthwhile to refinance in order to get a better interest rate. In our experience, it's usually a good idea. Remember when we talked about long-term thinking in Chapter 1? That's the idea here. Chances are you'll save more money in interest over the life of the loan than you'll pay in up-front costs to refinance.

Refinancing your mortgage means trading in one mortgage for another. You choose how much of the equity you've built up is to be included in the new mortgage.

If you've got a $100,000 home, and you've paid $50,000 of it off, you might refinance and get a new mortgage for $80,000. You've set yourself back, of course, but now you've got $30,000 cash to pay off those other debts.

This refinancing option can be a good idea if:

- The interest rate on your mortgage is higher than current prevailing rates.
- Your mortgage carries an adjustable interest rate that has been trending up.
- Your new mortgage loan is 80 percent or less than the value of your home. [That way you don't have to pay for PMI (private mortgage insurance).]

This option also has the benefit of consolidating your payments; you'll be writing only one check per month.

But there are drawbacks:

- You could be starting over with a new 30-year mortgage (that's why it's a good idea, if you can, to cut the term to 20 or 15 years).
- You could end up with a higher interest rate if your new mortgage carries an adjustable interest rate.
- If you borrow more than 80 percent of your home's value, you'll have to pay for mortgage insurance.
- You're freeing yourself up to borrow more. If you pay off all of your outstanding debt, you'll have plenty of room to borrow. The temptation to use this new credit can be overwhelming. If you don't resist it, you will end up in far worse condition than when you started.

We cannot stress enough the danger of using refinancing to pay off other debt. You could ruin your life if you aren't careful.

In the example just given, you've now got a new mortgage on which you owe $80,000 instead of $50,000, but you've paid off $30,000 in credit card debt. So far so good. But if you run up another $30,000 in unsecured debt, you've taken your bad situation and made it worse. You no longer have enough equity to cover your debt (and refinancing more than

80 percent of your home's value is a bad idea). You're back where you started, except that now you own far less of your home.

Refinance your mortgage to repay other debt only if you've made the commitment to stop borrowing and remain debt-free. If you can't resist the temptation to use more credit than you can handle, then don't run the risk of losing your home.

Debt Consolidation Loans

A debt consolidation loan is just a consumer loan that you use to pay off other debts. As with home refinancing, you're just trading one kind of debt for another.

There are unsecured consolidation loans, but by far the most common consolidation loan is a home equity loan. A home equity loan differs from refinancing in that your original mortgage isn't affected. With a home equity loan, you simply borrow cash against your equity.

Say your home is worth $150,000, and you still owe $100,000. That gives you $50,000 to borrow against. These days, lenders will give you up to 125 percent of your equity, so you'd get to borrow up to $62,500. We strongly urge you not to take advantage of this kind of offer; don't borrow more than your home is worth.

Let's say, in this example, that you borrow only 80 percent of your equity (a much more sensible option). You'd have $40,000 to pay off your other debts.

Is this worth doing? Financial experts disagree, but in general they advise against it. The truth is, it depends on you.

If you're paying interest rates of 15 percent or more on credit card balances, and you can borrow against a portion of your home equity at 8 percent, you're definitely going to save money in interest payments. (And the interest on the home loan may be tax-deductible, whereas the interest on the credit cards is not.) But there will be closing costs on the home equity loan; what impact they should have on your decision depends on how large they are. Reputable lenders will help you with this; it's in their interest to see you succeed.

The real question we want you to ask is, "Will this really conquer my debt?"

If you use a home equity loan to repay outstanding debt, you're giving up what you've accomplished in paying off your mortgage. The way we look at it, mortgage debt is better than unsecured credit card debt, so it's worth considering.

Home equity loans can be more expensive than refinancing your mortgage, though, so you should weigh your options carefully.

And, as with refinancing, if you then turn around and start using those credit cards again, you've probably just ruined your life.

That's why some financial experts will say that you should never use a home equity loan for day-to-day expenses. The odds are that you'll lose your house.

The bottom line is, consider a home equity consolidation loan to repay debt only if you're absolutely resolved not to return to your former habits and rack up new unsecured debt. A home equity loan is not to be entered into lightly. You're putting your most important asset on the line, and you'd better give the situation long and careful thought before you put it at risk.

And we must reiterate, do not borrow more than your home is currently worth. It's gambling, and it isn't worth the risk. Lenders are assuming that your home will increase in value; that's why they're willing to lend you more than your home's current value. But property values don't always rise. Prices can drop, the market can turn down, and you simply never know what will happen. Don't take a bad loan today on the hope that it will eventually turn good.

Unsecured Debt Consolidation Loans

An unsecured consolidation loan is very hard to get. If you can get one, it may be a good option. Start with your bank or credit union and see what kind of consolidation loan options it offers.

Consolidation loans are convenient, for one thing. Instead of writing 12 checks to cover all those credit card payments every month, you'll just have to write one.

Say you've got 12 credit cards with a total debt of $15,000. Your interest rates vary from 7 to 21 percent. If you can get a consolidation loan from the bank for $15,000 at an 8 percent interest rate, you'll probably be better off.

However, debt consolidation loans have some drawbacks. Like refinancing and home equity loans, they free you up to incur more debt. If you do, you're going to end up worse off for it.

Reverse Mortgages

A reverse mortgage or home equity conversion mortgage (HECM) is another kind of home equity loan available to homeowners over 62 who have built up significant equity in their homes. A reverse mortgage is a better option for senior citizens than the other home refinancing options just listed. If you think you qualify for a reverse mortgage, check with the AARP (www.aarp.org) or a HUD-certified housing counseling agency in your area.

Debt Settlements

Settlements are an increasingly popular way to take care of one's debts, but you should consider your options carefully before pursuing a debt settlement.

A settlement is simply a negotiated payment arrangement between a creditor and a debtor. The debt is resolved for an amount less than the actual amount owed, sometimes less than half the actual amount.

Sounds like a pretty good deal, right? It can be, but there are drawbacks. For one thing, your credit report will be adversely affected. Debts that are settled for less than the total amount owed are reflected that way on the credit report. It beats filing for bankruptcy or simply not paying by a long shot, but it's not as good as paying your debts in full.

Occasionally, individuals who have not made regular payments on their debts will receive an offer to settle directly from their creditors or from a third-party debt collector. These offers are made in good faith and are worth considering.

You may wonder why creditors would accept a settlement. Under normal circumstances, they might not. But if you've missed a few payments or have had trouble paying on time, your creditors may get the impression that you're close to filing for bankruptcy. When they're approached with a settlement offer, they may decide to cut their losses and accept a settlement. Better that than get nothing in bankruptcy court.

That's one of the reasons settlements are more successful when they are negotiated by a third party, like an attorney or someone from an accredited credit counseling agency. It reinforces the idea that a bankruptcy filing is at hand, and this is an advantage that you don't have if you try to negotiate a settlement on your own behalf.

One important consideration is that you have to have the available cash on hand to reach a settlement. If you owe $5000, a creditor may settle for as little as $2000—but you've got to have the $2000. The creditor is not going to accept payments for the next 2 years. Sometimes a third-party credit counseling agency can arrange for a series of payments, but they'd better not take too long; the creditor is already extending you a lot of leeway at this point, and creditors will bend only so far.

Settlement services vary in cost. Usually you pay a small up-front fee ($100 or less) and a percentage of the money saved. In our example, you've saved $3000; whoever negotiated the settlement for you might charge 15 or 20 percent of that amount.

Debt settlement can be a great way to repay a debt at a reduced cost; just be aware that your credit report will suffer a bit for it. How much? That's difficult to say. Evaluating credit reports is a complicated operation, but one thing is certain: Negotiating a settlement is not nearly as devastating to your credit rating as filing for bankruptcy.

One final caveat: There are disreputable settlement services out there. Many companies hang on to a consumer's payments for months until they've got enough to make a settlement offer. In the meantime, the consumer sees her or his credit completely ruined and perhaps gets sued. Check with the Better Business Bureau before giving your money to any settlement negotiator.

Bankruptcy

Bankruptcy protection is available to consumers who have no other alternative. That means that you should make sure you have exhausted all of your other options before you consider filing for bankruptcy.

There are some people, including most bankruptcy attorneys and the Consumer Federation of America, who seem to think that bankruptcy is perfectly fine as a first resort for consumers who are facing difficulties with debt. We disagree strongly; bankruptcy isn't good for anyone, neither the debtor who declares nor certainly our economy as a whole.

Remember, when a consumer files for bankruptcy, someone always pays. Bankruptcy is at best a necessary evil that should be used only as a last resort. Seek counseling from a legitimate credit counseling agency before you file.

Stay Out of Chapter 20

There are numerous kinds of bankruptcy. Chapter 7 is the most common for individual consumers. In Chapter 7, most types of debt are completely eliminated or liquidated, which is why Chapter 7 is sometimes referred to as liquidation.

The disadvantages of liquidation are many:

- It stays on your credit report for 10 years.
- It makes getting credit in the future difficult at best.
- Any credit that you do get will be incredibly expensive, with higher fees and interest rates.
- Alimony, child support, tax debt, and student loans cannot be discharged through bankruptcy and must still be paid.
- Filing isn't free; you'll have to pay hundreds of dollars up front to an attorney, which will weaken your financial position even further.
- Bankruptcy doesn't address the reasons that led you to file in the first place; there's nothing stopping you from going right back down the path to debt valley.

Chapter 9 bankruptcies are very rare; only a municipality can file for Chapter 9. If you happen to deal with a bankrupt city or county, you may have occasion to deal with Chapter 9. Otherwise, you'll never hear about it.

Chapter 11 is used to help businesses and corporations seek relief from debt. Also called reorganization, this kind of bankruptcy is complicated and shouldn't be attempted by amateurs. A lawyer who can handle reorganization will charge over $10,000 just to start the paperwork.

Chapter 12 bankruptcy specifically applies to family farmers; it's like a combination of Chapters 11 and 13. It's very rare, but if you have less than $1,500,000 in debt and at least 80 percent of that debt is farm-related, you can see an attorney about Chapter 12. Many creditors will look more favorably on this kind of filing than on a Chapter 7 filing.

Chapter 13 is the second most common type of bankruptcy filing. Unlike in Chapter 7, debt is only partially discharged, or not at all; instead, the consumer is given more time to pay off a debt while avoiding serious consequences like foreclosure. In order to file for Chapter 13, you'll have to show the court that you can afford to make the payments. This works for consumers who have just emerged from a hardship or returned to work after a period of unemployment.

Many people think Chapter 13 is less damaging to one's credit than Chapter 7. Not true. One isn't better than another; they're just different. Chapter 13 tends to be better for those who are trying to save their home, while Chapter 7 is recommended for those with mostly unsecured credit card debt.

Chapter 20 is our own facetious way of referring to a damaging practice of some bankruptcy attorneys. Consumers are sent down the road to Chapter 13 with little hope of success. A Chapter 13 plan takes 3 years to complete, during which you cannot begin to rebuild your credit. When the consumers fail to complete the plan, the bankruptcy attorney is there to help them file for Chapter 7 protection, which they probably should have done in the first place. The catch is, they have to pay the bankruptcy attorney twice; he's made double the money, and the consumer's recovery has been delayed by years.

The best way to avoid being a victim of Chapter 20 is to think carefully before entering into a Chapter 13 filing. Do your research, and, as always, consult an accredited credit counseling agency before you file.

COUNSELING

Many consumers seek counseling from third-party agencies and enter into debt management plans (DMPs) in order to pay off unsecured credit card debt. We've devoted a chapter to credit counseling. Turn to Chapter 5 for a more complete discussion of the credit counseling option.

Chapter 4

10 Different Kinds of Debt and How to Address Them

ADDRESSING 10 DIFFERENT TYPES OF DEBT

Each kind of debt is distinct and calls for different solutions. However, there are a couple of things that we feel are universal:

> *Education.* You can't know too much. The more you can learn about your situation, the better. Be sure to read the rest of this book to arm yourself with as much knowledge as possible.
>
> *Budgeting.* This is essential to conquering debt of all kinds. Don't skip Chapter 2 of this book if you want to truly master your personal finances.

As for the different kinds of debt you may have, here are some suggestions that will supplement everything we've told you so far.

CREDIT CARDS

The problem: Credit card debt is the worst kind of debt because, as we said before, it is designed to go on into the next millennium. It builds very quickly, but it goes down slowly. The interest rates are often outlandish;

the penalties, in the form of late fees, credit reporting, and so on, are onerous; and the companies are ruthless in applying them. This kind of debt is
very common; it's the number-one kind of debt discharged in bankruptcy,
and its popularity is only growing.

How you get it: By either spending more than you can afford or handling one too many emergencies with plastic.

Prevention: For one thing, shop around. Get a card that has the lowest interest rate possible. Ads for credit cards feature their convenience,
and that's exactly why these cards are awful. Leave them at home. Make
spending inconvenient. Try to keep it to emergencies. Pay off whatever
you charge right away, and don't buy anything you can't afford. *Never,
ever*, get a cash advance. If you do, transfer that balance to a new card
immediately.

If you really want to prevent credit card debt, think of it like preg-
nancy. It's fun to get into, but it grows uncomfortable in a mere 9 months,
and then it's around for 18 years or more. The best prevention is absti-
nence.

First step: *Stop*. Don't add another cent. Cut those cancers up. With
interest rates like theirs, they are growing enough without any help from
you.

Some points to consider when knocking out credit card debt:

- *Pay close attention to your interest rates.* Consider "balance surf-
  ing." Always be on the lookout for a better rate, and if you can
  transfer your credit card balances to a card with a lower rate without incurring fees, it's in your best interest to do so. You should
  always be striving to get the lowest rate possible.
- *Don't be afraid to talk to the credit card company.* We know that
  debt collectors can be harassing and unpleasant; don't talk to them
  if they are. But remember that the people from the credit card
  companies are just trying to do their jobs (and not very easy jobs,
  at that). If you don't have the money to pay them right now, calm-
  ly tell them so. Don't be pressured into making promises that you
  can't keep, and *never* promise to send them a postdated check.
  Sometimes the credit card company representatives will understand if you explain your situation to them. They may lower your

monthly payments for a time or work out a special payment arrangement with you. It can't hurt to ask.

What a lot of consumers don't realize is that you can sometimes get a better interest rate simply by calling the credit card company and asking for it. Try it; if your payment history isn't too spotty, the company may grant you a more favorable interest rate on the spot.

Apply these two principles when dealing with credit card debt:

- Pay the cards with the highest interest rates first.
- Keep making the same total payment even after you start paying off balances.

This last point is something that's built into the debt management plans negotiated by credit counselors. If your total credit card debt payments are $250 per month, keep paying $250 even after you pay off the card with the highest interest rate. Apply the extra money to the card with the next-highest rate, and just keep going until all the debt is paid. If you do this, your debt payoff will gain momentum as you pay off balances, snowballing until your last remaining credit card balance gets the entire payment each month.

AUTO LOANS

The problem: Reliable transportation is probably essential to getting back on track, because for most of us, our ability to earn—our entire livelihood—is tied to our car. Auto loans are double problems because they require full-coverage insurance, and that can add up fast. If the car is a lemon or goes off a bridge, you won't be able to use it, but you still have to make the payments. And unlike your house, it's worth less every month you own it.

Understanding it: First, find out exactly who lent you this money.

Car loans from a dealership carry heavy interest and the threat of quick repossession. These are the guys who say, "No credit, no problem; everyone approved." If you've got a loan like this, it spells trouble, and you need to find a way out. The exception to this advice would be if there is no other way, and you are using this loan only to reestablish credit after a disaster. If there is any other way, even cosigning, get that lower interest.

Finance companies that are part of auto manufacturing companies, like Ford Motor Credit and GMAC, are a little better. The rates will be more digestible, there is often a special deal for new cars if your credit is excellent, and occasionally, if you are aggressive enough, you can get a better deal on the asking price by making the company believe that it will more than make it up on financing.

The bank is the best way to go. For one thing, you have a trump card with some dealers. For another, repossession is more complex. Best of all, the rate will generally be better, and when the opportunity arises it will probably be easier to refinance this loan.

How you got in trouble: You overpaid, you wrecked the car, you lost a job, you had trouble with other bills. If you need a nice car in order to feel cool, you aren't cool anyway. Until you are in very good, very stable financial condition, cars must be transportation only. Not fun, not status, not cool; just transportation from one place to another.

Prevention: Shop exhaustively for the best deal, not just on the car, but also on the financing. Dot.com lenders that compete on rates are available now, but don't assume that because they beat their competitors online, they beat everyone. Nurture a healthy hatred for salespeople, don't get options you don't need, and remember that the best color for a car is "paid for." Paid-for cars offer the possibility of insurance savings because you can go down to liability alone. Take care of the car and take care of your driving record. Saving on a car includes saving on insurance, gas, tickets, and so on.

First step: You may be able to refinance your auto loan. If you've paid a significant portion of the debt, you can try to refinance the remaining portion over a longer period of time. This will extend the term of your loan, and you'll end up paying more interest in the long run, but it beats walking. If you got a dealer loan when your credit was hurting, but you've reestablished credit now, refinancing can knock off some percentage points. You're in real trouble? What can you get for it? Can you trade down carefully? Wash it, change the oil, list it.

If you get too far behind, you may receive a visit from the hated repo man. In many states, the lender on your auto loan can repossess your car without a warning, from any location. (The only exception is that it can't illegally enter your locked home or garage.)

How can you avoid a visit from the repo man? You might consider trading your car for a less expensive one. If you are having trouble making the payments, that's probably a sign that you have too much car for your income. If you can sell or trade in your car and get something less expensive, you can avert a crisis.

Whatever you do, don't hide your car. If the courts find that you intentionally hid your car in order to avoid repossession, they'll hold it against you later.

The best way to handle this situation is to act first. Call your lender and try to work out a solution. Many auto lenders will allow you to defer up to four payments over the life of an auto loan.

You may consider refinancing your home, if you own one, and using the equity to pay off your car. Don't enter into this lightly—it's better to lose your car to repossession than to lose your house to foreclosure—but if refinancing your mortgage can save your car without putting your home in jeopardy, it's worth looking into.

STUDENT LOANS

The problem: They are big, they last a long time, and many people end up doing something that has little to do with their degree or, worse, don't finish the degree, and end up paying on something with little value.

Many people get student loans from a family member. Obviously these are a little different. It's probably a little easier to be late, you probably got a good rate, and the rate is probably easier to adjust. These loans are also easier to default on. We advise against most family loans, especially for college. With some hard work, you can get the U.S. credit system to like you again. Aunt Mary just might hold a grudge forever. In the end, as bad as this sounds, if you have to default on someone, you'd rather rip off your bank than your mom. If you do borrow from family, take it seriously. Don't betray a trust by borrowing for school and then blowing off the history final. Families aren't as scientific, but they keep credit ratings too.

How you got it: Going to college.

Prevention: One thing is certain; don't take out more in loans than you need. A lot of students take out more than the cost of tuition so that they can live on the loan money, and most of the time students are eligible for extra. Don't do it; get a job. Millions before you have worked their way through college. If possible, take out less than the tuition. Is there a way to pay for some of that yourself? If you do get extra, don't spend it. You'll treasure that stereo more if you buy it with money you made. Apply any extra cash to next semester's tuition.

Also, don't be afraid to wait. Many people with student loan problems have them because they changed majors three times and took an extra year—or two or three. Frankly, almost every study shows that 20-year-olds who enter college having paid their own rent for a while do better than 18-year-olds fresh from mommy.

First step: Whatever you do, *do not* refinance a federal student loan with a private company. If you have a choice beforehand, always go federal over a private lender, including family members. If you are with a private lender, you are still not in terrible shape. Student loan debt, by itself, is the easiest to handle.

The first step in dealing with a student loan problem, as with any problem, is to identify it. With student loans, that may be tougher than it sounds because many people have several loans from different lenders or loan servicers or even loans with different guarantors. Take a while to find out exactly who owns your loan and exactly whom you're dealing with. Analyze exactly how much you owe, how much you are paying, and how much of what you're paying is principal and how much is interest. Can't figure out who owns your loan? You might try the National Student Clearinghouse Loan Locator. You can get it at www.nslc.org, and it can help you make sense of almost any lender that's part of the Federal Family Education Loan Program.

Now that you have a decent idea of whom you owe money to, how much you owe, and how much progress you are making or not making, the next step is to consider some actions.

1. *Direct payment.* If you aren't in serious trouble yet but could use a little relief, consider direct payment.

    Most loan programs offer an interest-rate reduction for direct payment. They will set up a monthly electronic withdrawal from your bank account. Sallie Mae, probably the biggest student loan provider/servicer, offers a 0.25 percent interest-rate reduction for direct payments. Others may do even better. MOHELA, which provides loans in Missouri, will give you a reduction of 1.75 percent. That adds up to some very serious money over a few years. Check your lender for its rate.

It's important to understand, however, that this doesn't make your payment any smaller. It just means you will be paying off more principal and less interest. That could take a few years off the life of your loan.

2. *Restructuring.* Most student loan lenders have fairly flexible payment options. It may help if you to restructure how your loan is paid back. One option is a balloon payment plan: You make smaller payments now and big ones in the future. Another option is lengthening the life of the loan. Instead of 10 years, you will now be paying for 15, but your monthly payment will be smaller. Both of these options can provide you with some immediate relief. Of course, they both result in your paying more interest over the life of the loan.

This can still be a very good strategy if you are smart and can keep to your budget. For the present, the extra money you free up must go toward other debts with higher interest rates. When that 14 percent credit card is paid off, you can shift that payment money back to your 7 percent student loan and hopefully knock a few years off its life. Once you are out from under the yoke of those other, nastier payments, you can restructure your student loan again and make real headway.

3. *Deferment or forbearance.* What's the difference? Basically, you can always get a deferment if you meet certain requirements. The lender gets to decide on a forbearance. In both cases, you get to put off paying on the loan, but your interest continues to build up while you are skipping those payments.

You have to apply for either one with your lender. You can sometimes get one because of unemployment or other circumstances; just be sure to explain thoroughly and truthfully why you are having trouble and exactly when you expect to get out of trouble. Another wise move is to ask for a partial forbearance. Explain that you can make a payment of 50 bucks a month right now, but not 90.

Don't ask for a forbearance if there is no end in sight. The idea here is that you get a break while you get your financial act together, get through a tough time, and get back on top. A deferment or forbearance will hurt you if it goes on too long, or if you can't pick up the payments at the end of it. Remember, nothing stops during a forbearance. You have decreased your monthly bills for a short time, but your debt is increasing, and in most circumstances the extra unpaid interest will be added to your principal and you'll now be paying interest on that too. Don't be shocked if your bill is higher at the end of the deferment or forbearance than it was at the beginning.

4. *Student loan consolidation.* If you have several student loans from different lenders or with different interest rates, consolidation is a solid strategy if you take the right steps. The first step is to apply for a federal consolidation loan. Federal loans are superior to private loans chiefly because this lender is easier to work with and because you can be sure that the interest is still tax-deductible. Be *sure* not to turn this loan into something that does not have tax-deductible interest.

If your application for a federal consolidation loan is turned down, shop for a consolidation loan from a loan servicer. The key word here is *shop.* Look at a least two, and again, make certain that the interest will remain deductible.

The advantages to this are that you can make just one payment, you lock in an interest rate, and you may be able to renegotiate payment structure in this way if your old lender wouldn't let you do so the other way.

What about That Tax Deduction?

It's a beautiful thing. If you make less than $55,000 a year, it's a full deduction. In other words, the interest you paid comes right off of your income. It really makes a difference.

Counseling Specifically for Student Loans

As we've said several times, there are many situations, and yours might need some special navigation. If it really is the student loans that are killing you, don't be afraid to get some help. There are a few counseling services that specialize in student loans. Be sure to shop around, though; look at more than one program, and do your best to get as much info as you can before you "buy" any. Be wary of "student loan counselors" who are really just there to arrange settlements or refinancing. You shouldn't have to be in default to get advice, and you shouldn't have to pay more than 40 bucks for it.

You might want to look at Student Loan Counseling Service at www.slcsloanhelp.com. This site offers a lot of useful information at no charge, and that's a good sign. You can reach the service by phone at 888-633-4850. Be aware that SLCS is owned by a collection agency, the CBE Group, but it seems to us to be on the level. Of course, before you enter into any agreement with anyone, be sure to read the advice about shopping for counseling in Chapter 5.

Home Loan/Mortgage

The problem: Mortgage loans are the most personal kind of debt. When your home is on the line, the problem is much more likely to have an emotional impact on you. The numbers are very big, too, so it's tough to get your mind around the situation and it can lead to despair quickly. The worst part of this problem is that it seems like it doesn't go away. You can't make your house payment? Even if you lose your house, you'll have to pay rent. It's a permanent bill, but it doesn't have to be a permanent problem. There are ways out.

Understanding it: What kind of home loan do I have?

The first kind of loan is an adjustable-rate mortgage loan. This means that the interest rate you are paying gets better or worse depending on the federal interest rate and interest rates in the world at large. This isn't a bad way to go if your income depends on the general economy—for instance, you own your own business, or you are a commission salesperson. The thinking is, when the economy is good, the rates will go up, but that's okay because people will be spending more with you, so you can afford it. When the economy goes south, the interest rates will too, so you can still afford it. The problem with this kind of loan is it's never an exact one-to-one relationship, and, more importantly, most people have jobs or salaries that aren't that dependent on the economy. Suddenly, people find that their interest rate has gone up, but their income has remained the same.

The second kind of loan is the fixed-rate mortgage. Your interest rate is locked in. Obviously that's great if the rate is low, miserable if it's high. Either way, there is an advantage in that it's easier to budget for.

Balloon loans, the third kind of mortgage loan, assume that you will make more money as you get older. Either payments start low and increase through the years or you are expected to make a large lump-sum payment at the end. For some people this works out well, but it could be a bad gamble. You have to bet that you won't be strapped by a layoff or a medical or legal crisis. A surprise baby could kill you with joy.

Another thing you need to be aware of is how private mortgage insurance (PMI) works. Simply put, lenders want to be insured against foreclosure as much as you do, but they pass the insurance payments on to you. In most cases, you will pay this insurance as part of your house payment, usually $100 to $300, until you have paid off 20 percent of your home's appraised value. This is insurance money, and it builds no equity. The key here is to get to 20 percent as soon as possible. You'll knock this insurance amount off of your loan payment when you do. Also, any kind of second mortgage or home equity loan that puts you back under 20 percent brings back the PMI. Likewise, loans that are back-loaded, like the balloon loans we discussed, keep you in PMI longer, so watch out for that too.

How you got in trouble: A mortgage problem almost always has little to do with bad spending and more to do with bad luck and bad choices. If you've got a mortgage problem, it's most likely due to unexpected unemployment, medical problems, or divorce.

Prevention: Prioritize. Don't make any financial decision that can affect or strain your home loan. If you are looking at your first one, look at all the options, the resalability of the property, and your job security. For any mortgage loan, think long-term and anticipate changes you may need to make. How many children are you likely to have? How might this neighborhood change? How secure is your job? Your spouse's job? Assume the worst and count on nothing.

First step: Check out the refinancing options. Budget carefully and try to make more cash and spend less. If your problems are really big, list your house right now. It's going to hurt if you take a loss, but that's better than losing it all. Trade down if possible; you can always go back up when your credit is better. Sharing a cramped bathroom in a smaller house with a teenage daughter is hard. Bankruptcy and foreclosure are harder.

We feel your mortgage should be your top priority every month for several reasons:

- *You don't want to be homeless.* If you stop paying your rent or making your mortgage payments, you could be out on the street. With the possible exception of IRS debt (which, in a worst-case scenario, can land you in jail for tax evasion), this is the most serious consequence of defaulting on a debt. Avoid it at all costs.
- *Your mortgage lender is your primary lender.* In almost all cases, you owe more money on your house than on any other single debt. This puts your mortgage lender at the top of your list.
- *Your home is your most important asset.* We always say that homeownership is an essential key to wealth creation. Homeownership should be everyone's goal, and if you own a home, your mortgage should be the first payment you make every month.
- *Your home can be the key to beating all your other debt.* If all else fails, you can consider refinancing. If you aren't making your mortgage payments, you can't refinance.

Mortgage lenders will help you if you get into trouble. Talk to them; the last thing they want to do is foreclose and throw you out on the street. Every mortgage lender will have a "loss mitigation" department designed to help prevent foreclosures.

The loss mitigation department may be able to help you work out a payment plan or restructure your monthly payments for a while. Maybe you can skip a mortgage payment in a tough month and make it up over the next three payments. Some mortgage lenders may even let you skip a payment altogether. Of course, remember that this means that you will be in debt longer and pay more interest on your loan.

Credit counseling agencies can also provide foreclosure prevention counseling. It should be free of charge, too. Ask the counseling agency if it's a HUD-certified housing counseling agency. If it is, then you're in the right place.

MEDICAL BILLS

The problem: You had some uninsured medical expenses. No one ever counts on that.

Prevention: First and foremost, avoid getting sick. Eat right, exercise, don't smoke, wear your seatbelt. Just as important, get good health coverage. If you can afford it, get supplemental health coverage as well. That Aflac duck is annoying, but supplemental insurance is inexpensive and worth it. Just be sure to shop around and get the best deal. Most of us get health coverage from our employers. Watch your employer. Demand the best service. Finally, check out your options thoroughly. Insurance payments hurt, but having no insurance kills.

First step: If you have outstanding medical bills and are having trouble paying them, remember two things:

- There's no such thing as debtor's prison.
- They can't repossess your health.

Of course we're not telling you to blow off your medical bills, but realize that the worst-case scenario here is a lawsuit; they're not going to take back that kidney they gave you.

Dealing with doctors and dentists can be unpredictable. Some may work with you to come up with a payment plan you can live with; others may demand total payment and threaten to call their lawyer.

Start by asking for the former. If you've prepared your budget, then you know how much you can afford to offer each month. Tell them you plan to send that sum every month until your debt is paid. They may decide to cooperate rather than incur the expense of an attorney.

If you fall too far behind or if your medical creditor doesn't want to deal with you, the creditor is likely sell the debt to a third-party collection agency. In this case, some damage has already been done to your credit rating; you might as well prepare to offer a settlement. Chances are the collection agency paid 40 percent or less on the dollar to acquire the debt and the original creditor charged off the balance. You can offer to pay the collector 50 percent or less—it's still making a few bucks, and it didn't have to work very hard to get it.

IRS/TAX DEBT

When you owe the Internal Revenue Service, you're going to have to pay. It's as simple as that. IRS debt can't be wiped out by bankruptcy except under certain conditions, and the IRS can impose liens and seize your assets. The bottom line is, you can't avoid your income tax debt.

Having said that, the IRS is flexible. It will work out a payment plan with you; just file a Request for Installment (form 9465) and you can break your debt up into payments over the course of 3 years.

The IRS may also be assigning penalties in addition to your tax debt. It's not difficult to get it to abate a penalty by reducing the amount or forgiving it entirely. Simply write the IRS a letter requesting abatement and telling your reasons for incurring the penalty.

Tax Liens

If you have a lien filed against you, you have to deal with it. You won't receive any tax refunds until the lien is satisfied, and you won't be able to buy or sell real estate until the lien is gone. There will also be a negative mark on your credit report for the next 10 years.

If you wait it out, a lien will fall off your credit report after the 10-year mark. The IRS can't collect after that, so the lien will be out of your life.

You can't borrow money to pay off a lien unless you can get the IRS to subordinate its lien, usually to a home equity lender. If the equity loan becomes the primary loan to be repaid if the property is sold, then a financial institution will lend you money even with a lien against you. But the IRS won't subordinate the lien unless it gets the money it's owed when you secure the equity loan.

Similarly, the IRS may detach the lien from some of your real estate (a lien makes selling property impossible because it's automatically attached to all of your real estate) and allow you to sell it, provided you pay off the IRS when you make the sale.

You can offer the IRS a debt settlement. As we said before, these are better handled by a third party, but you can try to do it yourself. Call the IRS and try to strike a deal.

If the IRS takes more drastic action, like garnishing your wages or imposing a levy on your property, you probably need the help of a tax attorney. If it's just you versus the Internal Revenue Service, chances are you're going to lose. Get some professional help.

CHILD SUPPORT/ALIMONY

The problem: These bills affect more than your credit record. You can be hauled into court over child support and have custody troubles or worse. The phrase "deadbeat dad" is thrown around everywhere these days—men who don't pay their child support are a favorite target of politicians, the media, lawyers, and so on. Of course, it's more complicated than they make it sound. Women are more likely to be delinquent in child support payments than men (of course, they're vastly more likely to have custody than the father), but "deadbeat dad" has such a nice ring to it that it's hard for reporters to resist.

Understanding it: It varies enormously from situation to situation and from state to state. Make sure the court and your lawyer explain exactly and clearly what is expected of you, how those payments can be altered, and what situations can affect them. Credit counselors deal with this issue often as well, but in that case, be sure you're working with an agency in your own state.

In general, child support is not something to be avoided or settled at a reduced rate. You can't declare bankruptcy to wipe out child support debt (although you can wipe out other debts and free up more income to pay your child support), and it's easy for your ex-spouse to garnish your wages to get child support money. If you're trying to fight paying your child support, you're probably going to lose.

Our advice is to keep lines of communication open and try to work out an agreement. Work to reduce your overall debt so that you can handle your child support payments more easily. Don't forgo paying off your other debt if you can help it, though; your overall financial health is as important to your children as it is to you, so don't drive yourself to financial ruin thinking you're doing what's best for them. Prepare a budget, plan ahead, and you'll get caught up on your child support in time.

As for alimony, it's something of an outdated concept. In general, these days alimony is awarded only when one spouse has been economically dependent on the other over the course of a long marriage. If you owe alimony, you'll probably have to pay it, but we don't think offering a settlement on a back-owed amount is inherently unethical. Every situation is different. You have to evaluate yours and make sure you do the right thing.

LEGAL DEBTS

Legal debts are rarely essential to your life—we'd never tell you to put them ahead of your mortgage, say, or medical insurance. But a lawyer is more likely to drag you into court and obtain a judgment, in which case he or she will be able to garnish your wages or worse.

Prevention: What can we say? Be careful and try to stay out of trouble. Have good insurance. If you've been wronged, see if there is some other way to deal with it besides court. Remember, in this day and age, lawyers are salespeople too, and they, more than anyone, are trained to prey on emotion. They will work you up and convince you that you have a case. Remember, a "legal consultation" is a sales pitch even if you are doing all the talking. Never agree to anything while you are in a lawyer's office. Go home, think it over, and call the lawyer back in the morning. Remember, too, that legal services are like anything else in that there is competition. Shop around. Get the best deal. Get a second opinion. Always compare, and trust no one who says "trust me."

First step: There are settlements to be had. Try to work them out before you do anything else. No one who paid a lawyer to get your money wants to pay another lawyer to garnish your wages. Get a settlement on your settlement.

The last people you want to be in debt to are lawyers. They're going to get their money, one way or another. Since they know the ins and outs of the system, they've got a distinct advantage over you. If you're in serious debt to a lawyer or law firm, you may need to find a lawyer of your own.

Lawyers are intelligent people, though, and they know they can't get blood from a turnip. They may listen to reason if you contact them and try to work out a payment arrangement. They also understand the realities of bankruptcy better than anyone, so they may be willing to settle a debt at a reduced amount rather than lose everything by forcing you into bankruptcy court.

PERSONAL LOANS

Most of us owe money to our family or friends from time to time. It's become more common these days for those of us in our twenties to rely on the "bank of Dad" for quick loans, especially for unplanned emergencies like car repairs.

Your family and friends are less likely to sue you, but that doesn't mean you should neglect your obligation to them. As with any debt, if you can't afford to pay it off, at least give them whatever you can afford. They'll be reassured that you haven't forgotten them, and they're more likely than any creditor to accept a show of good faith. The good news is that you (usually) won't have to pay interest.

Don't risk alienating those around you by neglecting your obligation to them. Your brother might be less likely to take you to court, but he may be more likely to beat the snot out of you if he thinks you have it coming (that's our experience, anyway).

Put personal loans on your action plan, pay what you can afford every month, always give something, and don't neglect to communicate. Many creditors, when dealing with proposals for a debt management plan from a counseling agency like Springboard, will request a "full budget proposal." They want to see where all the money is going before they agree to help someone by reducing interest or waiving fees. If the full budget proposal indicates a genuine need for a debt management plan, then the creditor will cooperate. You can provide your family and friends with a full budget proposal, too. Show them the budget you've prepared, let them know where the money is going, and they'll know you're not living the high life on their dime.

MISCELLANEOUS DEBT

Lots of debts defy categorization. Large business debts demand an entirely different book. Loan sharks and bookies demand a train ticket. As we noted earlier, there are a million ways to get in trouble and as many ways to get out. Whatever type of debt you're saddled with, what's most important is being sure that you understand just where you are in relationship to it.

Get answers to these questions:

How much do I owe?

To whom do I owe it?

How much interest am I paying?

What is my monthly payment?

Exactly how does this loan work? Fixed rate? Variable rate? Other?

How late am I?

How late can I be?

Can we settle? For how much?

What kind of refinancing is available?

What does that save me exactly?

Can I sell whatever I borrowed to buy? Can I just return it?

How can I change my budget to save enough to handle this? How can I change my budget to make more progress?

How can I make more income so that I can handle this?

Remember these general principles that we've outlined for the other debts:

- Prepare a budget.
- Communicate with your creditor.
- Try to work out a payment plan.
- Don't be afraid to ask for help if you need it.

Maybe you have some debts that aren't entirely legal. If you owe Tony Soprano for some old gambling debts, you could be risking more than a negative credit rating if you don't pay. Avoid borrowing from someone who collects debts at gunpoint.

Chapter 5

Credit Counseling

If you have serious debt problems, you may be considering credit counseling. This chapter will tell you what you need to know.

But first, try this on your own. Get serious about your goals and your budget, using whatever technique works best for you. Write all of your creditors explaining your situation and asking for a lower interest rate and lower payments. In this letter, be very respectful and polite, and explain your situation matter-of-factly; let them know that your only alternative may be bankruptcy.

These attempts may fail, but they are worth a try. Some creditors will respond by offering to put you into their own counseling services. Other creditors may just say no.

Still, you should try. If any of these things doesn't work, or if it takes more than 2 months, or if you can't make it another 2 months, come back here and learn about credit counseling.

The fact is, it isn't easy. It isn't easy to get a handle on your financial situation. It isn't easy to fight multimillion-dollar creditor giants. It isn't easy to ask for help or admit that you need it. It isn't easy to pay for help when what you need is more money. It isn't easy to feel confident that you made the right choice when there are so many different types of counseling agencies out there and so many shady characters thriving in them. However, there are some things you should know.

You should know that there are worthwhile agencies, too, and you can find them, and you can learn to tell the difference. You should know that they can help, if you find the right one. You should know that there is no shame in this. You should know that even if you do feel humiliated, the humiliation will last an hour or a week; bankruptcy lasts 10 years. That's why you should know about credit counseling.

WHAT CREDIT COUNSELORS ARE *SUPPOSED* TO DO

Obviously they are supposed to help you get out of debt and improve your credit. The way it works traditionally is that the counselor looks at all of your financial information and, after listening to your special needs, makes recommendations and creates a budget. Sometimes that's all it takes. It should be free or as close to free as possible.

If the counselor finds some serious problems, she has some tools at her disposal that can help you. The most common tool is the debt management plan (DMP). When a person commits to a DMP, the first thing he does is cut up his credit cards and agree to incur no new debt. Then he works out a monthly payment to the counseling agency. The agency uses this payment to pay the client's debt bills. The advantage to this is that the counseling agency has more leverage with the creditors and thus can negotiate better interest rates. That means that the client gets out of debt faster and with less pain. The secondary advantage is that the client now needs to make only one payment a month.

The final thing credit counseling agencies are supposed to do is offer education so that the client will learn more about money and debt and avoid problems in the future.

IT'S NICE IF THE COUNSELORS OFFER AN EAR AND BASIC HUMAN SUPPORT, TOO

The counseling agency must take in money in order to stay open and continue to offer this service, and it makes that money in a couple of ways. It charges the client a fee that should be enough to handle the servicing of the account. It charges a fee for the education part, too, but its main source of income is the creditors and something called "fair share."

The idea here is that the creditor would lose all the money if the client defaulted or declared bankruptcy. At least now the creditor is making *some* money, and as a thank-you to the counseling agency that made it possible for the creditor to avoid a loss, the creditor contributes a certain percentage of the payment to the counseling agency.

SOUNDS OKAY. WHY SO MUCH BAD PRESS?

Because so many agencies deserve it.

That does not mean, however, that all agencies do. There are distinctions, and it's important to make them. There are credit counseling agencies that are very good. There are some managed by the minions of Satan. As with anything else, there is a broad spectrum of service and quality to be found here, and neither blanket criticism nor blanket praise is the whole truth.

For starters, the DMP method is not the only way. For instance, some credit counseling agencies collect payments and hold them instead of distributing them to the creditors. The creditors eventually ask for settlements, and the company pays them off with the money it's saved up. This seems okay because the clients *do* get out of debt, but unfortunately this kind of debt settlement can destroy one's credit rating.

Some of the most famous counseling agencies charge very large fees, and many charge all of the fees up front instead of breaking them down monthly over the life of the plan. What's the difference? After those fees are paid, these companies have no reason to keep helping you.

A lot of counseling agencies, even some on the good side, pay bonuses to counselors who sign up clients for DMPs. That means that some people who may need only some budgeting help end up with payment plans. Worse than that, but similar, are nonprofits that, seeing that you aren't in such a bad situation, refer you to their for-profit spin-off. Or perhaps they see that you are in terrible shape. They refer you to a bankruptcy lawyer who gives them kickbacks.

Even an agency with its heart in the right place may be badly run or unstable. Some of these can manage to disburse funds only twice a month. Some are simply in financial trouble because of the decreasing amounts that creditors are paying in fair share. Financial instability threatens the payments you make to an agency and the agreements you have with your creditors.

So, yes, there are profiteers and scam artists in the credit counseling world and, yes, you have to shop carefully, but again, not every credit counseling agency is bad. If you do find a worthy agency, it can help you a lot. We'll tell you exactly how to shop smart and avoid rip-offs.

Bad Press They Didn't Deserve

1. *"Puppets of the fascist creditor regime."* A prevalent (and misguided) idea is that because credit counseling services get the majority of their funding from the credit card companies, they are "puppets" of the creditors. The truth is that the relationship between most credit counseling agencies (CCAs) and creditors is much more complicated than that. When the creditor reduces fair-share payments, the CCA jumps through the new hoops. It's less like puppeteering than like bullying. But a CCA can exist only if it helps both sides, so it takes the hits. Remember, the best thing about a CCA is its relationship with creditors, because that relationship is what enables it to make deals that you can't make. But yes, the funding comes from creditors; the debts get repaid, so the creditors pitch in because the CCA made that happen.

   The thing people must remember is that when the credit companies pay this commission, they also credit that amount to the consumer's account. They are partially subsidizing the customer's workout of his or her debts. If the intermediary (the credit counseling agency) got little or no funding from the creditor, it would have to get its operating cash from the client, just as bankruptcy attorneys, tax preparers, and other financial consultants do.

   Still, fair share smells bad to the public because it follows that all a CCA would care about is chasing debt management plans, because that's the only way it can get hold of any money. The problem is, this attitude assumes that enrolling people in DMPs is a bad thing. It certainly is not if a person needs a DMP.

   More importantly, a good nonprofit agency usually signs less than half of the people who come to it to a debt management plan. Some enroll as few as one-third. That being said, any agency that says it doesn't care about chasing DMPs is lying. It's how CCAs stay in business. Good agencies, however, realize that there are plenty of people who honestly need DMPs to keep them going and that they can help out those who don't need a DMP with some budget counseling.

2. *"It will kill your credit rating."* This is simply not true anymore. It may have been true at one point, but Fair Isaac Corporation, the company that calculates your credit rating, or "FICO score," has found that people on debt management plans or involved with credit counseling are a safe bet to pay back their loans, so Fair Isaac has stopped using counseling information in the calculation of the FICO score. Fair Isaac states plainly that credit counseling will not affect your credit rating.

Counseling will be mentioned on your credit report, and it is possible that some lenders will view it as negative, though many will not. Once your DMP is finished, your debts are paid in full, and your credit report will reflect that.

I UNDERSTAND CREDIT COUNSELING NOW. DO I NEED IT?

Every service will give you its own quiz with a "Did you answer yes to five or more of these questions? Then you need help" ending. The fact is, if debt payments are becoming a problem, you should look into it. The good agencies will help you make the right decision anyway.

If debt payments are making things impossible, don't wait. If you really aren't sure, here are a couple of those quiz questions that really do matter.

Are you using one card to pay off another, or any monthly bill, for that matter? Then start shopping for credit counseling. Are you counting on something that probably won't happen to solve your debt worries (book deal, recording contract, lotto, court settlement, inheritance, and so on)? We won't tell you to give up your dream, but you probably want to be a little safer just in case. Check out credit counseling.

Basically, if you have any debt concerns at all, it doesn't hurt to shop around and see what's available, as long as you shop smartly.

Do I Have to Be Delinquent?

The simple answer is no. There are no accredited counseling services that will not see you if you are not delinquent. There are some creditors who will not give you a break on interest or restructuring if you are not delinquent, but a CCA can help a lot with these creditors, too. When you tell a creditor that you need a break or you will file for bankruptcy, the creditor may or may not believe it. When a CCA tells creditors this, it carries a little more weight, especially if it's a reputable agency. If your credit is still good but you are quickly approaching the brink of disaster, don't wait. Your chances of beating any kind of problem, from health, to relationships, to money, are better if you identify the problem early and start working on it.

That's why a good CCA can help anyone. It may only be able to refer you to a bankruptcy lawyer, but at least you tried everything and you found out the facts.

HOW TO SHOP FOR A REPUTABLE CREDIT COUNSELOR

There are always Internet and phone offers. We looked into several spam offers that came to our email unsolicited and didn't find any that met our criteria. The safest bet is to ignore all email offers or anyone who calls you at home offering their services. It's almost a general rule of life that the good stuff you have to look and work for; the bad stuff comes to you.

That being said, where should you start looking?

Accreditation

The idea behind accrediting bodies is that they do the research for you. They set up standards and accredit organizations that meet them. Accreditation isn't fail-safe, but it is definitely the first thing to check. If a CCA is not accredited, pass on it. But what if it is? What does that mean, and which accreditations are worth noting? Here's some insight.

1. *NFCC.* The National Foundation for Credit Counseling is an organization of credit counseling services that has specific requirements for membership. NFCC members must be non-profit and must offer free or low-cost counseling and financial services. Most of the members are called Consumer Credit Counseling Service of Somewhere: North Carolina, Springfield, Phoenix, and so on.

    The NFCC seal means that the CCA's business practices are at least passable, and that it is genuinely nonprofit. What is really good is that it usually means that the agency won't force a debt management plan on clients who simply don't need it. But the best thing about NFCC agencies is that the independent accrediting body they use is COA.

2. *COA.* All NFCC members are accredited by the Council on Accreditation of Services for Families and Children Inc. (COA). COA focuses specifically on social service programs, and that's why it knows exactly what it is looking for. COA is international, not-for-profit, and independent, but most importantly, it's rigorous. Here are a few of the standards we particularly like. Apply them to your search yourself.

The agency must be bonded, licensed, and insured, and must meet all consumer disclosure requirements as set forth by the FTC. The agency must offer "a variety of deposit options, including electronic methods" and the "immediate correction of improper posting." The agency must make disbursements at least twice a month. (We recommend at least once a week. Springboard and a few others disburse payments every business day.) Clients must receive, at minimum, a quarterly statement, and, best of all, for an agency to be accredited by COA, clients must be encouraged to increase deposits if they can so that the debt goes away more quickly. This prevents agencies from even thinking of keeping your debt hanging around so that the fair share they receive hangs around.

All of these are excellent criteria, and there are plenty more. The most significant is the strict governance that comes with COA accreditation, in particular the way it heads off private inurement. Inurement of various types is rampant in non-COA-accredited counseling agencies. The CEO of the counseling service may own a for-profit business on the side that receives referral business from the nonprofit counseling agency. In some cases it's the CEO's wife or brother who owns the for-profit, but it's all about skimming money off of the counseling agency and putting it into the CEO's pocket. COA agencies don't engage in this kind of self-dealing.

That's why we recommend that you don't work with any CCA that is not COA approved. When it comes to accreditation, this is simply the top of the line. We also recommend that you keep in mind that COA is good but not perfect. Feel safer, not safe. You still need to shop.

You can shop the NFCC at www.nfcc.org. It can give you the info you need on NFCC members located near you.

3. *AICCCA*. AICCCA stands for the Association of Independent Consumer Credit Counseling Agencies, and it works much like the NFCC. It too is an organization of different agencies, banded together for more lobbying power with creditors and regulators. To join, an agency must be accredited and meet a set of standards similar to those of COA.

    Two of AICCCA's standards that we especially like are, "Debt management plans should be established only when they are appropriate, and advantageous to the client," and especially, "No creditor will be excluded from a DMP unless it is beneficial to the client." The idea here is that an AICCCA agency can't say, "We don't do student loans" or "We can't help you with that credit card company." There is some wiggle room, but you should definitely be sure to enforce that idea.

    If an agency is AICCCA, it should help you with a creditor whether it expects any fair-share money or not. Go to the AICCCA site at www.aiccca.org and print out the standards, and remind the agency of them if you have to.

4. *ISO 9000*. AICCCA agencies are accredited by a body called ISO 9000. We like it less as an accrediting body for credit counseling agencies than COA. It's inferior in this area, and here is why.

    ISO 9000 is an international accrediting body set up originally for manufacturing companies. It's a manufacturing standard that has been stretched to apply to a wide range of business activities. COA, you will remember, is specifically for social services. Being accredited by ISO 9000 means, basically, that your agency has met the same standards as a factory in Mozambique. Its sheer inclusiveness should make it apparent that ISO 9000 is a very general standard. In fact, ISO focuses on producing measurable outcomes and on "say what you do and do what you say." The content of what you say isn't really important—it's the fact that you do it that matters.

5. *The Better Business Bureau.* Besides being an AICCCA or NFCC member (or, if possible, both), the agency should have a clean record with the Better Business Bureau. Negative information here is an immediate no, but a clean record should not mean yes. The BBB can be settled with, and some pretty dubious agencies find that it's easier to just pay off BBB complaints than to stop their questionable practices. So please, don't take a clean BBB record as a plus; just take it as a minimum.

   You can contact the BBB through its web site, www.bbb.org; it has a handy "check out a business" function there. The web site can also help you locate contact information for your local BBB. You can get the BBB by phone at 703-276-0100 during business hours.

6. *Housing and mortgage counseling: HUD certification.* This is pretty straightforward. Do not get mortgage counseling from any agency that is not HUD-certified. If you have a mortgage problem, try to find an agency that is both NFCC- or AICCA- and HUD-certified so that it can do everything at once. If you can't find an agency that is both, go to the mortgage counseling first. It may even recommend a CCA that it trusts or that will work with it.

7. *The creditors' recommendation.* The fact is, most large creditors are checking out counseling agencies for themselves. More and more the agencies have to prove to the banks that they are trustworthy. If you have one serious credit card debt in particular, it may not be a bad idea to ask the creditor which CCA it recommends. If the CCA you shop can't help you with your Bank of America card but another CCA can, that's a good sign.

Know Your State Laws

Some major CCAs were making a lot of money by keeping their clients' first payments as a "voluntary" contribution. The state of California stopped this by putting a cap on the amount of money a CCA could charge for credit counseling and education. As a result, some of the more dubious national agencies pulled out of the state.

If you're shopping for counseling by phone, you might start off by hinting that you're from California. If the agency says that it can't help you if you are in California, you know it is probably charging its clients too much.

In a way, California has become an accreditation for national counseling services by itself, and other states are following suit. If your state has strict licensing of CCAs, then you'll have some protection against profiteers.

Most Importantly! (Beyond Accreditation)

Accreditation is only the first step. Once you have found a few agencies that pass this initial step and decided whether you need face-to-face, Internet, or phone counseling, now it's time to do the most important thing you can do.

Compare. Here is a rule for all major goods and services, lawyers, insurance, travel agencies, Realtors, whatever: Shop two; decide at home.

Say it out loud. "Shop two; decide at home." Salespeople don't want you to leave the office without a sale; some counselors feel the same way. Take advantage of the counseling. If the counselor adds it all up and says you need a DMP, ask some questions, tell him or her that you'll consider it, and go to the next place.

Your competing counselors may come to the same conclusions and give the same advice. This is good confirmation. They may also give you very different advice. Now you have a second opinion, and you can take the best budgeting help from each one. Whatever happens, commit to nothing in someone's office or on the first phone call. Go home, talk it over, sleep on it, and make a good decision. Don't go with the counselor you liked best; go with the one who made the most sense. Whatever you do, don't get pressured and don't let any agency make you believe that its way is the only way. Shop two; decide at home.

Ten Questions to Ask Your Credit Counselor

So you've got two agencies that have been accredited and have certified counselors.

While you're there, ask your counselor a few questions. Here are some recommendations:

1. *Do you get a commission for signing DMPs?* Actually, most counselors do, and it's not a major indicator, because even reputable agencies give these commissions. What's important here

is that you ask the question. It puts counselors on their guard and makes it less likely that they will sign you for the wrong reasons. It also makes it much more likely that they will give you clear and exhaustive reasons why they think a DMP is right for you.

2. *What fees does your agency charge?* All counseling should be free of charge and confidential. Meeting both of those conditions is getting trickier. A lot of the Internet-based CCAs may offer free counseling, but they'll turn around and sell your information to as many marketing firms as they can find.

As for debt management plans, you currently shouldn't have to pay more than $20 per month to be on the plan. There may be an enrollment fee as well; this shouldn't exceed $100.

3. *Does your agency have any local branches I can go to for help?* This may depend a bit on your personal preference, but many people feel better off with a counseling agency with offices that they can visit in person. CCAs that counsel only by phone or over the Internet may not offer the kind of personal service you need.

4. *Does your agency provide any education programs or support for me while I'm on a debt management plan?* Make sure that there is some educational component to the DMP. A true service agency wants to help you address the problems that led to your debt in the first place.

5. *Will your debt repayment program handle all of my debts?* Often a nonaccredited agency will work only with debts to creditors who will contribute to it. Debts owed to creditors that don't financially support an agency (such as state and federal tax debts, student loans, and collection agency accounts) are put back in your lap to handle on your own. Watch out for agencies that "cherry pick" like this—your best interests are not on their mind. Your agency should work with all creditors for those debts that can be placed on a debt management plan (including housing issues, judgments, and liens), whether those creditors contribute to the counseling agency or not. (Sometimes you may be asked to handle a small balance on your own for purely administrative reasons, but be sure it is up to you.)

6. *How safe is my personal information?* Make the agency convince you.
7. *Do you sell mailing lists?* If they sell your name or address to outside parties, say no and walk.
8. *Will you help me with my questions even if I'm not on a DMP?* An AICCCA or NFCC agency should.
9. *Are your counselors certified by an independent third party?* Accredited counseling agencies put their counselors through rigorous certification programs; make sure that anyone who counsels you has had to prove that she or he is qualified for the job. Be wary of CCAs who certify their own counselors ("Counselors at Oxford Credit Counseling are certified by Oxford Credit's Certification Program!").
10. *Do you get paid for referrals?* This isn't always a bad thing, but at least apply the rule. If the agency sends you to a bankruptcy attorney, you still need to shop two and decide at home. Just because you trust your counseling agency doesn't mean that you should trust its lawyer. If you find out that an agency has a referral quota, keep shopping.

In addition to these questions, even if the agency is accredited, it doesn't hurt to ask whether there is a minimum amount of debt it handles, how often it disburses funds, and what the counselor's actual qualifications are.

It also makes a lot of sense to write these questions down and check them off. Perhaps leave room for some notes. Even if you don't take any notes, look like you are. It's good to have counselors believe that they will be accountable for what they tell you.

In conclusion, we think that if you take these steps, you will be able to avoid the bad apples in the credit counseling barrel; but even so, if you feel uncomfortable, don't be afraid to get out of there and shop some more. If an agency does you wrong, report it. The fewer bad apples, the better.

Feeling scared by all this? Don't worry. You can do it. Lots of people have good help. You might be more worried now than you were before, but the truth is, you know more, too. Read this chapter again, find some other opinions, and make the best decision you can. You'll make the right one.

Chapter 6

A Closer Look at Credit

WHAT IS CREDIT?

Credit, simply stated, is using other people's money.

More precisely, it's having *access* to other people's money. When you have *used* other people's money, you have debt.

This may sound simple, but many people don't make the connection between credit and debt strongly enough. All credit is a loan, and most often the lender is a bank. When you swipe that plastic, remember that you're going into *debt*.

A credit card is supposed to be a convenience item. It takes the place of cash, so that you don't have to carry cash around with you. It allows you to order things by phone or online. Unfortunately, most credit card users don't limit their borrowing to convenience. Most of us use credit cards to live beyond our means. When credit is abused in this way, disaster usually isn't far behind.

When you think of credit as access to debt, the importance of having good credit comes into focus. If your credit is good, you have ready access to debt. With good credit, you can borrow right now, and you'll have more choices in lenders. Bad credit reduces your access to debt and limits your choice of lenders.

"Good," you say. "Debt is what's gotten me into so much trouble. I'm better off without it." Yes and no. You're probably better off without the unsecured debt you've racked up, but the student loans and the mortgage are worth it. Remember, the reason to rebuild good credit is that it provides access to the good kinds of debt.

YOUR CREDIT REPORT

Lenders will pull your credit report before they offer you a loan or credit. What they're looking for is some indication that you are a safe bet, and your credit report contains most of the information they need in order to make that determination. In the simplest terms, your credit report is a record of how you pay your bills.

There are four major credit bureaus, and you're likely to have a credit report on file with the first three of them:

> Equifax
> Experian
> TransUnion
> Innovis

Once upon a time, there were more than three thousand credit bureaus. Now there are really only three. We'll discuss Innovis later.

What Your Report Says about You

The different bureaus' credit reports are basically the same in that they contain certain information about you:

> *Personal information.* Your credit report will contain your name and your current address, and also your last few previous addresses. Your recent employment history may be on your credit report as well. Your mother's maiden name may be there, and your social security number will definitely be there.
>
> *Inquiries.* Every time your credit report is accessed, the inquiry will be noted on your credit report and will stay there for 2 years. A lot of inquiries over a short period of time may indicate that something's amiss. Personal inquiries, such as when you or a

prospective landlord or employer accesses your report, will not count against you.

Public information. If you've been sued in court and lost, the judgment will show up on your credit report, as will bankruptcies and tax liens.

Credit information. This is the heart of the credit report. Any open credit accounts that you have are indicated here. If you've been more than 30 days late on any debt payments, you'll receive a negative mark on this part of the credit report for each delinquency.

Your statement. You are entitled to add a personal statement of 100 words or less to your credit report. Typically, this will be in response to a negative notation that can't be removed any other way. It's also a good idea to add a "victim's statement" if you've suffered from identity theft.

Because of all the personal information on your credit report, it is a very sensitive document. If your credit report were to fall into the wrong hands, that person would have everything—your social security number, your credit card numbers, everything. Please treat your credit report with the utmost care. Keep it someplace secure, and don't discard it without shredding it.

Why Your Credit Rating Is More Important Than Ever

Many people live most of their adult life without ever seeing a copy of their credit report. This must change. More than ever, in our society, a person's credit report is the measure of that person's character. Landlords check it to make sure you'll pay the rent. Employers check it to see if you'll be a stable and trustworthy employee (you can understand how an employee who is drowning in debt could be perceived as a greater risk for theft or embezzlement). We've even heard of graduate schools checking credit reports to see if an applicant is a strong finisher (and whether the applicant is likely to repay her or his student loans).

The bottom line is, everything important that you do these days—getting a job, buying a car, buying a house, getting an education—involves someone checking your credit report.

How to Get a Copy of Your Credit Report

Generally, we advise consumers to check their credit report once a year. You may check it every 6 months if you're in the midst of correcting and rebuilding your credit. We also advise anyone who is preparing to apply for a major loan to check his or her credit reports at least 6 months in advance; that gives you time to make any necessary corrections and possibly increase your score.

Your credit report will cost you around $9. The amount varies from state to state, but plan to spend around that. Actually, we advise everyone to get his or her credit report and FICO score (see "Your FICO Score"), which will run about $13. That score is what's really important, and it's worth the extra four bucks to get it.

You can order your credit report from each of the three major credit bureaus by visiting their web sites:

www.experian.com
www.transunion.com
www.equifax.com

A good site from which to order your complete credit history and your FICO score is www.myFICO.com.

If you prefer, you can call the credit bureaus to order a report:

Experian: 1-888-397-3742
TransUnion: 1-800-888-4213
Equifax: 1-800-685-1111

And finally, you can order your reports the old-fashioned way, by mail:

Experian
National Consumer Assistance Center
P.O. Box 2002
Allen, TX 75013-2002

TransUnion Corporation
Consumer Relations Center
P.O. Box 10000
Chester, PA 19022

Equifax Credit Information Services
P.O. Box 105873
Atlanta, GA 30348

Whatever Happened to TRW?

Many consumers may remember their credit report being called a TRW report. TRW Information Systems is still around; it's just changed its name to Experian.

The Fourth Credit Report

Experian, TransUnion, and Equifax offer basically the same service, but your reports from those three bureaus won't be the same, and neither will your three credit scores. You never know which report a particular lender is going to use, but for a large loan like a mortgage, a lender will check all three of your credit reports.

As we mentioned earlier, there is a fourth credit report, Innovis. It doesn't report your credit information to lenders, landlords and employers won't pull its report, and you'll have to do a little digging to find it.

Innovis Data Solutions provides information to creditors who are compiling mailing lists. The idea is to cut their costs by screening out those consumers who have blemishes on their credit report; that way, institutions can send information only to those people with top-notch credit and avoid offering credit to higher-risk consumers.

In one way, a negative Innovis report is kind of a bonus: It means that you get less junk mail. Nonetheless, you may want to see your Innovis report and make sure that there are no surprises on it. Innovis asks that consumers request their report in writing:

Innovis Consumer Assistance
P.O. Box 1358
Columbus, OH 43216-1358

For more information, you can visit Innovis online at www.innovis-cbc.com.

OPTING OUT

We strongly advise you to call this number and opt out of prescreened credit offers:

> 1-888-5 OPTOUT (1-888-567-8688)

This same number covers all four credit bureaus. After you call and opt out, you won't receive any more preapproved credit offers.

"But wait," you say. "I *like* receiving preapproved credit offers!"

First of all, we doubt that you really exist. And if you do, we're sorry, as much as you love junk mail, it's time to take credit offers out of the mix. If you are the kind of person who responds to these things, that may be part of the reason you're having difficulties with debt. Call the number.

YOUR FICO SCORE

All consumers with a credit history (about 260 million of us) also have a credit score. Fair Isaac Corporation pioneered the use of credit scores, and its FICO score is the one most lenders use.

A FICO score is a three-digit number between 300 and 850. The higher the score, the better, and anything over 700 is typically considered "good" credit. The score takes into account various information on your credit report and is calculated using top-secret algorithms.

What Fair Isaac Corporation will tell us is the importance of certain information to your score:

> *Payment history* is the most important factor, accounting for 35 percent of your score.
> Second most important is your *amounts owed,* at 30 percent.
> Third is your *length of credit history,* at 15 percent.
> Then *new credit* and *types of credit used* come in at 10 percent each.

Obviously, the best way to improve your FICO score is to make all of your payments on time and in full, and to pay down your balances.

The interesting thing about credit scoring is that it doesn't take your income into account. It's possible for a multimillionaire to have a credit score of 400 and a minimum-wage truck-stop waitress to have a score of 800. It all depends on how they pay their bills. This may seem odd, but FICO scoring has proved to be remarkably predictive; the higher your score, the more likely you are to repay your debts. It's as simple as that.

DISPUTING AND CORRECTING YOUR CREDIT REPORT

You can legally dispute any inaccurate or outdated information on your credit report. You simply write the credit bureaus a letter requesting that they remove the information in question. By law, they have 30 days to investigate. If they find the information to be accurate, they'll leave it on your report. If they can't prove that it should stay, the law says that they must remove it.

We'd provide sample dispute letters in this book, but we don't think it's necessary for two reasons:

1. When your order your report, the credit bureau will send instructions on how to file a dispute.
2. Disputing your credit report is easier than ever. These days, you can dispute information through the credit bureaus' web sites without ever having to lick a stamp.

With 260 million consumers to keep track of, it's amazing that the credit bureaus don't make more mistakes than they do. If you do happen to have an inaccuracy on your report, dispute it immediately.

As for outdated information, 7 years is the statute of limitations for most things. Anything older than that must be removed by law. The big exception is Chapter 7 bankruptcy, which stays in place for 10 years. All negative information is automatically removed from the report after the appropriate time limit; it's rarely necessary to request that a credit bureau remove it.

When Your Record Is Permanent

If you apply for a large amount of credit (over $150,000) or a large life insurance policy (also over $150,000), the creditor or insurer has a right to see your entire credit history from its inception. This is also true of employers when you are applying for a job that pays over $80,000.

CREDIT REPAIR—A VERY DANGEROUS PRACTICE

You may have heard of credit repair companies that promise to provide you with a completely fresh credit history. These "credit doctors" charge hundreds of dollars ($400 seems to be the going rate for this service) and basically commit fraud.

We don't like using the phrase "credit repair" because of its connection to these companies. We prefer "credit correction," because that's all you can legally do—correct inaccurate or outdated information. If the information on your report is legitimate, it has to stay on for the full term of 7 or 10 years. If you try to have it removed earlier than that, you're committing fraud.

Credit repair clinics use a couple of fraudulent tactics:

File segregation. The credit doctor helps you get a new social security number or EIN (employer identification number), with which you can start a new credit history. This is illegal and fraudulent.

Frivolous bombardment. Since by law the credit bureaus have only 30 days to investigate your dispute, credit doctors will flood them with correspondence, sending them so many dispute letters that they have no hope of completing their investigation in time. They're then forced to remove the disputed information. This is also illegal.

"But," you ask, "doesn't it work? Won't I have clean credit?"
For a month or so, sure. But there are two problems to consider:

You're the criminal. The credit repair company doesn't put its name on the dispute letters it sends. It puts yours. Legally, *you* are the one who committed fraud.

It doesn't last. The creditors who put the negative information on your report in the first place still haven't been paid. They're going to keep putting the negative information on your report until you pay or settle, or until the legal deadline for reporting the account comes. Just because the credit repair company got you a completely fresh credit report doesn't mean that it's going to stay that way.

"How do they get away with it?" When we tell consumers that credit repair is illegal, they always ask that question. The truth is, many of us get away with things that are illegal every day. Jeff disagrees with seatbelt laws and violates them every chance he gets. He's been getting away with it for years. Just because someone gets away with something doesn't make it any less illegal.

LEGITIMATELY REESTABLISHING YOUR CREDIT

You can rebuild your credit legally and legitimately. It won't happen overnight, but it's not as hard as you think.

Do It Yourself

Anything legal that a credit repair company can do, you can do yourself. Disputing the inaccurate or outdated items on your credit report is easy— why pay someone else hundreds of dollars to do it for you?

A legitimate nonprofit like Springboard may offer a service like our Credit Report Review and Correction Service, where the agency helps you write legitimate dispute letters for things that truly don't belong on your credit report. This can be an important help to people who are dealing with a complicated report, but it's still a convenience service; you're paying us to do what you could easily do yourself.

So why would we offer the service if you can do it yourself? There's a lot of nastiness out there, that's why. We've seen banks misreport people's credit deliberately. They might report someone's account status, but leave out the credit limit. They do this to lower the consumer's credit score so that she or he will be less likely to qualify for another loan and take her or his business elsewhere. We're trained to sniff out, dispute, and correct this kind of thing. Legally and legitimately.

Once you've gotten rid of the stuff that shouldn't be on your report, you'll have to deal with the things that should be there.

Here are the most important steps in rebuilding good credit:

Make your payments on time every month.
Don't incur more debt.

Follow these two rules, and your credit will improve over time, guaranteed. Even when there is negative information on your report, your score will improve. This is because the older the information on your credit report is, the less it counts against you. Time heals everything.

If you've got negative information on your credit report that's relatively fresh, it's important that you get caught up on those accounts and work out a payment plan with those creditors. If you read the information on settlements in Chapter 3 and want to go that way, that's fine, but remember that it won't be as good for your credit score as paying your debts in full.

If you have old accounts that you haven't touched in over 5 years, consider just ignoring them for another 2 years and letting them drop off your report. If you send them any kind of payment now, you "reset the clock" and the information is re-upped for another 7 years. The time limits on your credit report are from the date of *the last activity* on the accounts in question. Remember that when deciding which items to address first.

This sounds a bit unethical, doesn't it? It is. The best policy is to repay all of your debts. We'd advise you to pay the recent ones first, but eventually you'll probably have to deal with the old ones. Sometimes creditors sell old accounts to collection agencies after the 7-year mark has passed, and then the collection agency may be able to report your account for another 7 years. Unfortunately, that negative information doesn't always go away when it's supposed to.

If you have an old account that's already in collection, there's another reason to leave it alone: If you make contact with the collection agency, you let that agency know that you're alive. Collectors will start calling, day and night, until the account is paid. Don't reach out and invite all that stress and harassment into your life unless you have the money and are prepared to pay off the account.

Don't Close Old Accounts

Since the age of your credit history is a factor in your score, it's a good idea to keep old credit accounts open. That old department store card that you haven't used in years can seriously improve your credit rating; as far as the credit-scoring algorithm is concerned, that's an account that's been in good standing for a long time.

The other important point is that closing an account won't make it go away; it'll still appear on your credit report as a closed account. It's better to have an open account with the potential to boost your score.

Don't Open New Accounts

It's a bad idea to run around and open new accounts just to boost your credit. You could end up with a lower score—remember, length of credit history is important, and too much new credit is detrimental. Concentrate first on keeping your existing accounts current.

If you don't have any open accounts, then it's a good idea to try to get some credit in order to prove you can handle it. If you can't get approved for a credit card, talk to your bank about a secured card. You'll need to tie up some money in a special savings account that you won't be able to touch, but there's no way you'll be denied the secured card.

For example, you put $500 in savings. You are issued a credit card with a $500 limit. There is no risk to the creditor, because it will just take your savings if you don't pay (don't let this happen—your credit will be devastated). Then you use that credit card normally, paying off your balances in full every month. After 6 months of that, the bank will probably give your $500 deposit back and make the card a legitimate unsecured credit card. You've just established credit.

Sometimes it will take a year to establish the account this way. The important thing to know is that credit ratings are reported in 6-month increments. Say you buy a refrigerator on credit from a department store with the intention of paying it off quickly in order to build your credit. That's a good plan, but make sure you pay it off over at least a 6-month period. If you pay it off too quickly, it won't be reported at all, and you will receive no benefit.

The bottom line is, have credit and use it responsibly, and you'll see a dramatic increase in your score every 6 months. The old accounts will hurt you less, and the recent ones will really help.

Chapter 7

Banking

THE UNBANKED

Not having a bank account is a problem for many people. Around 10 percent of American households are "unbanked": They have no account with a financial institution. This is of concern because "fringe banking," the alternative to bank accounts, is expensive. Check-cashing, payday loan, and pawn establishments all cost more money than a bank. Money orders cost more than checks, and finally, there is the risk of theft, which could cost a lot more than a safe bank account.

There is some good reasoning on the other side of this controversy, too. The main argument is that overdraft fees can destroy you, and this is true. People who have serious trouble with checking accounts and fear another bounced check find that they are safer with cash-up-front transactions like money orders.

Another issue is inconvenient hours and locations. Some people need banking late at night. Many low-income neighborhoods have seen banks move out and check-cashing businesses move in. If it's going to cost you $2 and an hour to take the bus to your nearest bank branch, isn't it worth the fee to get your money on the corner?

Some research has also suggested that many banks simply make low-income and minority customers feel very uncomfortable. That is certainly a valid issue in your decision making.

SO WHAT SHOULD YOU DO? AND WHY?

Despite these arguments against traditional banking, it's still in your best interest to get a checking account if you can. Fringe banking simply costs more than regular banking in every instance. Extra costs are obviously no good for people who are in debt trouble. That goes for the extra costs in time, too. Going someplace to get a money order, standing in line at the post office, waiting for the grocery clerk to print it—however you do it, reaching in the drawer and pulling out a checkbook is faster. Just be careful not to let that convenience get you into trouble.

A word about money orders: They aren't as safe as most people believe. The first reason is that they don't stand up in court. A money order receipt does not prove that the right person got the money or cashed the order. This means that an unscrupulous landlord or creditor can cash the money order and then claim that you never paid, and you have no way to prove that creditor wrong. Checks, on the other hand, are legal proof in most cases.

Second, some money order companies are unstable. The failure of General Money Orders in Los Angeles in 1992 left many people who had paid their bills facing eviction, utility shutoff, late fees, and credit problems. If you have to use money orders, get them from the post office.

The first possible solution for the unbanked is the "lifeline" accounts that many states require banks to offer to low-income families. If you can get this deal, take it. This kind of account has no minimum balance. The disadvantage is that these accounts also have limits on the number of checks you can write and rarely offer linked ATM cards. If you might be eligible, check with a couple of banks to find out if your state has these accounts or not and what it takes to get one. Check more than one. Some banks may not want to talk about it.

BUT I CAN'T GET A CHECKING ACCOUNT AT ALL

Despite efforts by state and federal agencies, it's getting tougher rather than easier to open a checking account. You have to pass two tests. The first one is ChexSystems, and the second is your credit report.

ChexSystems

ChexSystems is the primary account verification service in the United States. It works like this: If you mishandle your bank account, you get listed on ChexSystems. When you apply to open a new account, the bank checks your information with ChexSystems. If ChexSystems says you messed up, the bank says no, and you don't get an account.

If this happens, the first thing you need to do is get a copy of your ChexSystems report. Get your ID info together and call ChexSystems at 800-428-9623 or write a polite request with your name, social security number, and address to ChexSystems Consumer Relations, 12005 Ford Road, Suite 600, Dallas, TX 75234. ChexSystems can also be reached online at www.Chexhelp.com. The report costs $8.50, but you are legally entitled to a free copy if a bank turned you down because of a ChexSystems report in the last 2 months. If this happened 6 months ago, just go to a bank and get turned down again. It will take only a few days, and it will save you $8.50.

When you get the report, look it over very carefully. Check it against your old bank statements if possible. If you find something that you're sure is wrong, make a copy of your report and highlight the items you are disputing. Write a letter explaining that the information on the report is erroneous and send it to Dallas (you can fax it to 972-242-4772).

It will take a month for ChexSystems to investigate and notify you of anything it found. If it does see it your way, it should take the mistake off your report immediately. Check your report often until the problem is remedied. If the investigation showed that you were right, but the problem is still listed 2 weeks later, call ChexSystems and remind it to clear the problem. Now you can apply for an account again.

If the ChexSystems report is accurate and you did botch a bank account somewhere, there are still some things you can do. First, talk to the bank in question and find out if settling the problem will be enough to get it to fix the report. Most banks will say no, but some will help you and contact ChexSystems if you just pay them what you owe them. Only the institution that reported an incident to ChexSystems can have it removed if the information is accurate.

Get Checking

Another option that is spreading across the country is the "Get Checking" program. With Get Checking, you take a class about banking and receive a certificate upon completion. It's a bit like traffic school for checking accounts. You take the certificate, which shows that you've learned how to handle your account better, to a participating bank or credit union, which will allow you to open an account even with negative information on your ChexSystems report. So far, people who use the Get Checking program have had a high success rate in managing their checking accounts after graduating.

Get Checking isn't free; most places that offer it will charge around $50, and you'll be required to pay off any outstanding items on your report. To find out if the program is offered in your area, visit www.aboutchecking.com.

ChexSystems also serves as a collection agency, so if you can't find the original bank to which you owe the money, or if you've moved away from where you had the trouble, you can make your payment directly to ChexSystems.

News Flash: Life Isn't Fair

One thing we see repeatedly is a tendency on the part of banks to use ChexSystems reflexively as a punishment for customers who have made mistakes. Ideally, ChexSystems is about helping banks avoid risk, but we've seen banks put negative information on a ChexSystems report in order to get back at a client who didn't pay a safe deposit box fee on time. Many of the 7 million consumers who have been reported to ChexSystems have had similar experiences. Unfortunately, there's little one can do about it. At the very least, don't enter into a banking relationship with a financial institution that uses ChexSystems as a form of retribution. If you know of a bank like that, tell everyone you know not to bank there.

Apart from trying to persuade the reporting bank to update your ChexSystems report or completing the Get Checking program, a third option for those with negative ChexSystems information is to talk to a branch manager when applying for a new account. You see, ChexSystems makes no judgment about you in its report; it simply provides factual information. It's the banks that decide whether or not to deny you an account based on your report, and they have total discretion. A branch manager can always elect to grant you an account regardless of your ChexSystems report. Unfortunately, unless the branch manager's your uncle, it'll rarely happen. For most branch managers, that's too big a risk.

Finally, you can try to find a bank that doesn't use ChexSystems. Good luck; 80 percent of all banks use it, and all of the major ones do. Some of the financial institutions we've seen that don't check with ChexSystems are rural banks in small towns and banks that require a high minimum balance to open an account. There are some places where you can buy a list of non-ChexSystems banks for $25 to $50, but the lists we've seen are outdated, inaccurate, and not worth the price. (One list we saw offered ten banks in our state; three of them *did* check with ChexSystems, another would open accounts only for active military personnel, and the other six were 80 miles or farther from our location.)

Credit Reports and Checking

As well as checking ChexSystems, many banks will also check your credit report. If your report looks bad, so will your chances of getting a bank account. If this is why you are being turned down, then the first step is obvious: You have to get that credit rating back up.

IF YOU *HAVE* TO REMAIN UNBANKED

Perhaps you are getting there, but it's going slowly, and it will be a few months before you regain access to a checking account. Perhaps your situation is very bad and you are going to need a few years. Here are some ideas.

First, try getting a savings account. Most banks will cash a check for you if you have any type of account with them, so a savings account can save you on check-cashing fees. Many savings accounts offer ATM access, so it's still fairly easy to get to your money. Savings accounts are safer than mattresses, plus, they earn interest, even if the rate is miserable (it will be). There are minimum balances for opening most savings accounts, but shop around. Some places don't require them. There are still community banks that will let children open savings accounts for $10; you just have to find them. But remember, banks don't like it when you treat a savings account like a checking account. If you dig into that account too many times in one month, they'll probably start charging extra fees.

Second, if you can't get a savings account or your savings account doesn't buy you check-cashing privileges, get a friend or family member with an account to cash your checks for you. You can sign your checks over to that person and, with a little hassle, get your cash. If you can find someone you trust thoroughly, you can save a lot on check-cashing fees. If it's possible to take this further without any problems for your helper, there may be some checks that he or she can write for you. Just be certain that this is a person you can trust.

Finally, if the problem is just minimum balances, you may want to look into online accounts. Most of them have much lower minimum balances than traditional banks. The problem there is that unless you can get direct deposit, you'll have to mail everything. Obviously this doesn't work if you're a waiter or someone who deals in a lot of cash.

I'VE GOT AN ACCOUNT; WHAT DO I NEED TO KNOW ABOUT IT TO GET OUT OF DEBT?

If you are doing okay with regard to credit, debt, and money in general, there is plenty of banking research you should do in books wider in scope than this one; but if you've got a debt problem, you have to reexamine the way you handle money as a whole. Banking is part of that picture.

Keep Costs Down

Next to no one actually uses "bank fees" as a budget category, and yet the fact remains that banking costs money. Do whatever you can to keep your banking costs low. For many people, that begins and ends with being careful. You've got to understand and consider your bank fees. Don't let them sneak up on you. That $5 service charge may be the difference between a good check and a bad one if money is tight. So find out exactly what you are paying and what it's for, and then plan for that outlay.

Next, be very careful with your account. Overdraft fees are double traps: You have to pay the store extra, and you have to pay the bank extra. A bad check for five bucks can cost you a hundred. Debit cards are especially dangerous because many people don't write down their debits or withdrawals in their check register. Your card clears a purchase, and then that check you sent off 5 days ago hits the account and decimates you.

Write down your debits in your check register. Do it! At the very least, get obsessive about exactly where your cash is. Some people check their balance every single day. Whether they do this at ATMs or online, it gives them a mental picture of precisely what's in that account.

Finally, don't forget those automatic debits. It can be very convenient to have your utility bill deducted directly from your account each month, but people with serious debt problems often need a little more flexibility. Being able to adjust your billing timetable by just a couple of days can help you avoid disaster. People with banking problems often forget that that money is coming out of the account on a certain date. Be careful. Don't slip. Bounced automatic debits carry the same huge fees as returned checks.

Banks and Accounts

Choosing the right bank and the right account for your needs can help you expedite the process of getting out of debt. Here's a quick overview and a few recommendations.

First, here's a quick review of just what banks do. Banks use your money to make money for themselves. They offer either a service, like checking, or interest on a savings account to get you to invest your money. Then they use that money to make loans or occasionally just invest it better than you did. This doesn't sound so good, but in reality it's great because the safety and services are worth it. Just remember that banks are competitive businesses, so please, whatever kind of account you are looking for, shop around. Get all the information and find the best deal.

Kinds of Banks

National banks, savings banks, state banks, and savings and loan associations all function in basically the same way. The main difference is really who regulates them: the federal or state government, the Comptroller of the Currency, or the Office of Thrift Supervision. In any given city, the differences between the accounts offered by these types of banks will be slight but worth checking out.

The main difference may be the service. Some large organizations never want to see you at all, and may even charge a fee for talking to a teller. Smaller banks are easier to deal with, but a lot less convenient. If you are going to be around for a long time, consider finding a bank with people who will be around for a long time. In many small towns, there are banks with officers with whom you can really build a relationship. When you work out your first home loan with someone, and then talk to the same person about your kid's first car loan 15 years later, loyalty usually buys you something. Small banks depend on that loyalty to stay in business. At big banks, officers regularly move from branch to branch. Your paper history still means something, but your handshake history is lost.

The Credit Union: An Exception

Credit unions aren't technically banks, but they serve the same basic functions without the frills. Originally credit unions were designed to serve a specific group of people, Johnson County teachers, for instance. But credit unions are getting easier to join. Unlike banks, credit unions are nonprofit and are "owned" by their members. What does that mean? Good things.

It means lower fees, lower minimum balances, higher interest rates on savings accounts, and lower interest rates on loans.

Credit unions are also just as safe as banks. The National Credit Union Share Insurance Fund insures accounts to $100,000, just as the FDIC does for bank accounts.

What could possibly be the disadvantage?

The real drawback to credit unions is lack of convenience. Credit unions are definitely shorter on hours and locations. Weigh this against your needs, but our opinion is that credit unions are usually worth the trouble.

Shopping for a credit union is convenient, however. Simply call the Credit Union National Association at 800-358-5710, or look at its web site, www.cuna.org, to find a credit union that you are eligible to join.

WHAT IS THE BEST CHECKING ACCOUNT FOR SOMEONE WITH CREDIT TROUBLE?

"The cheapest one" is an answer that makes sense, but there is a lot of play in that line. What you really need to reel in is the *safest* one. Many checking accounts have lower fees if you carry a big minimum balance, but people with debt problems often have trouble keeping a thousand dollars or more in their accounts and wind up paying more fees than usual. Even if you have the thousand bucks right now, it may be in your interest to go with an account that requires no minimum so that you can push money around more easily. Remember, even with interest-bearing checking that pays an amazing 2 percent, you're losing money if you have debts building at 8 percent.

We recommend that you prioritize this way: safety, expense, convenience. Once you're out of trouble, you can move convenience up on your list.

WHAT ABOUT SAVINGS?

This is actually a little more complicated. It's true that at most banks, a regular savings account will pay very little interest, but one of your goals is to be safe. That means getting an emergency fund to protect your credit. As we've said before, 3 months' salary is an essential goal. Unemployment, health, and auto emergencies can't destroy you once you get there. Unfortunately, that money has to be reachable. A regular savings account pays very little interest, but the cash is ready when you need it.

Money market accounts pay slightly better interest, and they usually offer a few checks, too. The money is still available, but you have to maintain a minimum balance.

Certificates of deposit pay even better interest, but they are the least flexible. With a CD, you agree to place a specific amount of money in the bank for a specific amount of time. The more years you agree not to touch the money, the better the interest rate. The problem is, if something comes up and you have to get the cash out, you are charged substantial penalties.

People with credit problems need to think of these accounts as a stepladder to stability. Get your 3-month emergency fund up to speed in a regular savings account.

Once it's there, use extra money to pay off any high-interest debt. That's the investment you need to make first, but if you're doing that easily, or if you're down to debts that you can handle, a money market account is the next step up. Keep the savings account! But when you have the cash for the money market minimum, add that too. Now you have two places with emergency money. You should be feeling pretty good.

The next step is reading another book. There is a ton of good investment advice out there. Most of it is not too favorable to CDs. There are savings bonds, Treasury bills, mutual funds, stocks, IRAs, and other options, each with different tax advantages and possibilities. If you are making your debt payments and you have an emergency savings account, a checking account, and a start on a money market account, then you've really made it out of your debt pit and back to sea level. It's time for you to start looking up and researching the best way to use your money to climb.

ATM AND DEBIT CARDS: WHAT THAT VISA LOGO MEANS

ATM cards allow you to withdraw cash, check your balances, and make deposits at automatic teller machines. Some stores will let you use them for purchases and even give you cash back. You just put in your PIN there at the checkout counter. The money comes out of your checking account.

Debit cards are just ATM cards with a credit card logo, Visa or MasterCard. They work slightly differently. You can use these cards to buy things at any place that accepts regular Visa or MasterCard cards. All you have to do is sign the slip. Again, this is not a loan: The money is taken from your checking account.

The advantages of these cards all fall into the category of convenience. You don't need as much cash. You can get cash when you do need it. The bank doesn't have to be open for you to make deposits or transfers.

The main disadvantages have to do with convenience, too. For one thing, it's convenient to spend money that is in your account tonight, but was meant to cover the check that the electric company will be cashing tomorrow. *Be careful* with your card. The amount shown on the ATM screen is *not* your balance. Your balance is the one in your check register that shows how much money you've sent out in all of those outstanding checks. Please be sure not to spend money you've already spent just because the check hasn't shown up yet.

The second "convenience" disadvantage is that the ATMs of other banks are always right where you need them. These days, it's all about double billing. The bank that owns this machine is charging you a fee. It will tell you so right on the screen. Say, 2 bucks. That seems okay to you because, hey, you need the gasoline, right? But your bank more than likely will charge you a fee as well, because you used someone else's machine. That's another two bucks. Now that $20 worth of gas has cost you $24. Do you look for the best gas prices? Take the time to look for your bank's ATM machines, too. Take note of which grocery stores have your bank's machines.

Some people note the convenience of ATMs for travelers. They forgo traveler's checks, thinking that there will be ATMs wherever they are going. Yes, there will be, but will they belong to your bank? Traveler's checks still cost less than double ATM fees. If you have to use an ATM on the road, get all the money that you will need at once. Two transactions for $40 each might cost eight bucks. One transaction for $80 costs only four.

Finally, convenience goes for crooks, too. Debit cards don't demand PINs, just signatures. That makes them easy for everybody to use, including the guy who just stole your card. When your card is missing, report it immediately. The sooner you report it, the less of that thief's big-screen TV you are liable for.

ONLINE BANKING

Online banking is a pretty good deal for people with debt problems. Just like credit unions, online banks offer higher interest rates with lower minimum balances. It's easy to check your balance every day right along with your email. These banks also make it a little tougher to get to your money, which could be a good thing if your spending is hurting you.

The problem is, unless you have direct deposit, you have to mail in your deposits. They have *got* to get there on time so that you can get your bills paid without late fees.

As with anything else affecting your money, shop and compare carefully before you choose an online bank. Bankrate.com can point you to a number of Internet-based banks. Be sure to find out if the bank is FDIC insured. If you can't tell, call the FDIC at 800-934-3342. (Psst. Shhhhh. Bankrate.com has a lot of other good info, too. You might want to spend some time there if you go.)

Chapter 8

Surviving the Journey

Mental, emotional, psychological, attitude—whatever you call the problem, debt wreaks disaster on your brain. In the United Kingdom, psychologists are naming syndromes and being trained to deal with debt-related emotional problems. In America we may be a bit behind in this area, and at Springboard we are certainly not psychologists; however, there are a few emotional aspects of debt that we see every week, and we'd like to address them in a basic way. If debt stress is eating a hole in your stomach lining, then by all means see a professional therapist. If it's just keeping you awake—or, more likely, keeping you in bed because it's so hard to face—then you might start here.

Counselors seem to agree that there are three big psychological issues when it comes to debt: denial, despair, and the task of getting your brain ahead of your spending.

DENIAL

There's no problem with anything—your car, your gut, your relationship, your job, the feng shui in your closet, anything—that can be solved until you recognize it. We're going to assume that you are past denying your debt problem, since you've bought this book, but often it isn't that simple.

Perhaps you see it, but your spouse doesn't, or your kid doesn't, or your mom doesn't. Sometimes you just have to build a case.

Get the evidence together. How much debt do you have? How long will it take to pay off? What things have you planned for that are in jeopardy now? It's not quite an intervention, but it may feel like it. If nothing else, get that denier to a credit counselor. No one has to sign up; just get a diagnosis. Whatever you do, don't start denying it yourself. Get that credit lump looked at before it grows into something you can't cure. Please.

DESPAIR

The first defense against hopelessness is recognizing it for what it is. Whenever you find yourself thinking, "I may as well buy it. I'm never going to get out of debt anyway. What does it matter?" that's despair. Why not just give in? Max it out and look toward a settlement, a bankruptcy, or a fake identity in Mexico.

Here's why: because none of those things will bring the sleep back or halt the ulcer. Debt limits your freedom just like being tied to a chair, and bankruptcy, settlements, and life on the lam are just more ropes with tighter knots. You will never get free in one fell swoop. You have to work every day to make your bonds looser. Twisting, chaffing, trying—it isn't much fun, but thousands of others, with bigger debts and tighter ropes than yours, have done it, and as bad as it hurt, they made it through.

There is only one effective way to handle despair: take action. Once you feel that you're doing something, no matter how little, you start to feel that you have a chance. If you think your situation is hopeless, focus on a tiny goal first. A small success could snowball. If you fight off despair a few times successfully, it gets easier. And that's the best thing to do about despair: just take action. Any action.

That's not helping? That's okay. We know someone who can help.

Debtors Anonymous

Debtors Anonymous is a group that is dedicated to helping people in both practical and emotional ways. Some people have found everything that they need in order to get out of debt with Debtors Anonymous. Others have used it in tandem with credit counseling or other plans. The main thing is, when you are dealing with debt despair or debt denial, DA is very helpful because the people you will meet at DA are people just like you. They have been there, and their motivational stories are that much more motivational because they will look you in the eye and shake your hand when they tell them.

DA works a lot like the other "Anonymous" programs. It's been described as "a twelve-step program with paperwork" because in some chapters, the members provide one another with a lot of help on budgeting, goal setting, reading your FICO report, and so on. DA does a great job at helping people to face their debt problems and stay strong against despair. What DA does an even better job of handling is our next topic of discussion, controlling your spending.

Debtors Anonymous knows that controlling your spending is one-day-at-a-time job for a lot of people. It is there to help you examine and beat the spending habits that led you into debt in the first place. If you just can't stop accruing debt, please give Debtors Anonymous a call.

You can find a Debtors Anonymous chapter near you by checking out the organization's web site, www.debtorsanonymous.org, or calling the DA general services office at 781-453-2743.

THE BIG ONE: CONTROLLING YOUR SPENDING

Here is a fact: The majority of American households have a pizza cutter.

People wonder why many foreigners think Americans are soft. This is why. Americans have lost the ability to cut pizza with a knife. Americans are no longer tough enough to put a pan of oil on the stove; they need a Fry Daddy. A broiler pan is far too complex for us, and the extra 15 minutes is unbearable, so there is just no alternative to a Lean Mean Grilling Machine. We know a man who, even though he was in danger of losing everything, continued to buy Coca-Cola and name-brand cigarettes. He was just not tough enough for Shasta and GPCs. He certainly was not tough enough for water and gum. We know an uncle who was losing his house—in his garage was a riding lawnmower, a weed eater, electric hedge clippers, and an edger. Losing his house was an option for him. Cutting the hedge by hand was unimaginable. We've watched a woman who complained about money problems every single day walk right by a 69-cent loaf of store-brand bread to buy a $3.79 loaf of Orowheat.

There are many practical ways to control your spending, but at the heart of any method that works, there has to be a fundamental value shift. Being tough, in our opinion, is a value that has been lost. In the end, controlling spending is about being tough—toughing out the lack of a cappuccino machine, toughing out the lack of an electric can opener, toughening up on salespeople and advertising.

A person in a debt crisis has to make pride a fundamental value—pride in endurance, pride in toughness. People who successfully make radical changes in their spending have the same mantra repeating in their heads: "I am tough enough to do without, and I'm proud of that."

I can do without; I can do without; I can do without. In the grocery store, I can do without. At the discount store, at the car lot, at the bank, I can do without. With the utility bills, with the telemarketers, watching TV, at the gym, in the restaurant, in the movie theater, in the book/furniture/clothing store, in the gift shop, in the video shop, in the smoke shop, I am tough enough; I can do without.

Do I really need a Roll-a-Hose? A special pasta spoon? Name-brand perfume? The clapper? Is it true that they can break any American by simply cutting off her or his air conditioning?

Learn to separate Needs from Wants, as we said in Chapter 2. Find out how many things you can do without. Take pride in the growing list, and be tough. You can do it. Many people who thought they were hopelessly soft have grown some calluses after all. We believe in you, and in us, as Americans. Your toughness has a point. Someday, if you can just be tough enough now, you'll be debt-free, and then you can have all the electric toothbrushes you want.

Now that the motivational rant is over, what are some practical ways to control spending?

The main weapons in spending control are still budgeting and goal setting. Sticking to your budget in a disciplined way is all-important. Keeping what you really want in your mind will help keep you away from things that you only temporarily want. But there are some other little psychological helpers too.

Allies

The more friends and family you can get on board with your new goals, the easier the process will become. Remind each other that you are tough; you can do without.

Make It Harder

One reason that overspending is such a problem is that it's so easy. Anything you can do to make getting to your money or credit more difficult might be a good thing. First and foremost, if you have a consumer debt problem, cut up those cards right now. Any counseling service would demand it. People put up many excuses—I need it for emergencies, what if I have to rent a car, long-distance reservations, and so on—but the truth is, you don't need it nearly as much as you think you do, and you won't be sufficiently motivated to get that emergency fund underway until it's made truly necessary by the lack of a credit card safety net.

The second thing you can do to make getting to your money harder is to leave your buying power at home. That checkbook or credit card has to stay in the lockbox when you go to the mall. This way, if you see something you want, you have a chance to decide whether you still want it in a saner atmosphere. Your kitchen was not designed with the sole purpose of inducing you to buy things, the way a store is. Leaving your money at home gives you the opportunity to ask yourself whether this item is worth it.

Lists, Lists, Lists

Successful people write down their goals and make lists of the things they need to accomplish each day. Spending might be the most sensible place of all to employ the list.

Don't go to the grocery store without a list. Grocers perceive the list as their natural enemy. Grocery stores are specifically designed to get you to buy things that are not on your list. End caps at the end of each aisle are set up to tempt you and almost never have anything that you would have put on your list.

Beware of those end caps; they usually look like they're offering some kind of bargain, but they rarely do. As a rule, don't get taken in by flashy displays or boldly advertised prices. Just because a price is written in great big numbers doesn't mean it's a good one.

One of the grocer's main sources of profit is snack foods: chips, pretzels, and soda. That's because the markup on a loaf of bread, something that probably would be on your list, is next to nothing, while the markup on nacho ranch tortilla chips can be as high as 200 percent. Are Doritos on your list? No. That's why the snack aisle is probably one of the biggest, most spacious, most colorful, end-capped, retailed, sale-bannered places in any grocery.

Having a list is the best defense against buying things that you don't really need. If it isn't on your list, don't buy it. Again, the store is designed to make you think you need something. Decide what you need when you're at home, a place designed for common sense.

Lists Go for Everything

Discount stores are a good place to get cleaning supplies and light bulbs and other day-to-day items. They have these things at much better prices than the grocery. The problem is, they have everything else, too. *Stick to that list.* These places are masters of retail and marketing. Their displays can make dirt look like a basic human need. (Thom's actually bought potting soil he didn't need.) The aisles are arranged to spit you out in tempting places. Think about it: Why aren't all the aisles just up and down? It would be so much easier.

They don't want it to be easier. They want it to be a pain to find what you are looking for, so that you have to walk past more stuff, with more sale tags and more displays.

Make your list before you go to these places, and look neither to the left nor to the right. Get your items and get out of there. Remember, the store is the enemy. This is the battlefield. If you keep to your list, you win.

Again, you can do this. When you make a list, write that on the top: "You can do this."

Take It Back

Some people have found that they get control after they get home.

Springboard's CEO, Dianne Wilkman, does this, in a practice she calls "shopping bulimia."

"Sometimes I realize that a cashmere sweater just isn't on my budget," Dianne tells us. "I take it back to the store, and if the clerk asks if there was a problem with the merchandise, I just say, 'I realized that I can't really afford it.' It's surprisingly empowering."

The lesson is, don't be afraid to take things back. You can still fix things if you hurry.

MORE ABOUT SAYING NO

Those Nasty Salespeople

Everything over $10 seems to have a salesperson attached. It's important to remember that salespeople have been trained by the dark side to use their special powers. We want to give you a couple of sales basics to recognize and stay away from. When you know how you are being manipulated, escaping is easier.

Admen and salespeople use every kind of propaganda technique, from bandwagon ("all the winners drink this; everybody wears that"), to testimonial ("Shaq likes Burger King"), to card stacking, to repetition ("I've heard of Oxy-Clean, it must be good"). But the hands-down number-one propaganda device used in sales and advertising is name-calling.

Not the obvious type: "Brand X bites" or "My opponent in this election hates puppies." No, we mean the subtle, insidious type of name-calling where they call *you* names.

"Are you feeling flabby? Can't fit into those old jeans? Do you not look like the impossible model we're showing you in this commercial right now? Is your family not the happy, intimate, close, supportive circle of love that this one is? Is your car not as cool as this family's or this guy's? Is your house/lawn/face/chest/stove/floor/laundry/air/mind/sex life/whatever ugly? That's because you are inadequate and subpar. That's right. You suck. The only answer is this ionically charged bracelet, pheromones, and breast augmentation."

Advertisers and salespeople know that people who feel good don't buy stuff. They have got to make you feel bad. Bad, bad, bad—while smiling. Once you feel inadequate, you'll need a suggestion for filling the gap. Their product is just the ticket.

Remember that everyone is trying to break you down. The worse you feel, the more you'll spend. Don't give in. You're all right. You've made some money mistakes in the past; so what? You're still great.

Not buying that? Convinced you really are flabby? Well, maybe so, but for God's sake, don't let some Madison Avenue hawker insult you like that.

What gives that person the right to point it out? If you can't battle this kind of bull with good self-esteem, then at least battle it with indignation. See through the lies. A lot of those models hate themselves, too. All those happy children in those perfect families are actors with greedy, loud-mouthed, divorced stage moms, and you know it. At least your kids aren't being paraded in melting greasepaint for 5 hours a day in front of the hundred-degree klieg lights. Your family is probably just fine. All it needs is for you to get out of debt, and you can, if you stay strong during the commercial break.

1. *Salespeople sell themselves first.* Salespeople generally try to be likable. They will always start with a smile. This is the beginning of what they call "the impulse curve." They have planted the seed of a positive feeling. Now they are going to make it grow into excitement. They want to talk to you, get to know you, make it seem like we're all friends here. They are not your friends.

2. *They are going to ask you questions designed to get you saying yes.* The more you say yes to anything, the more the momentum builds. "Nice day, huh?" "Yes." The salesperson has just scored a point. Your "impulse" is building.

3. *Card stacking.* Now that we're friends and you are saying yes, the next step is to build value. Commercials do this too, but this is really the "card-stacking" propaganda technique. You are told one great thing after another, but never the negatives. Every "card" or piece of information we deal you seems better than the last, and look how many there are! Then, when we finally hit you with the price, wow, it doesn't seem so high.

4. *Urgency!* Above all, salespeople want you to think that this is your last chance. Tomorrow, there will be none left. This price is good only for today. When I walk away from your door, this deal will never come to you again.

   Salespeople operate with the motto "be-backs mean no greenbacks." They can't let you out of the store, out of the showroom, off the phone, off your porch, without that sale. "It's got to be now. While supplies last. Act now." Urgency.

   This, of course, is crap. The truth is, if a product is good, it doesn't need such salespeople; the public will seek it out. If a person isn't willing to let you go home and think about it, it's because there is something that that person doesn't want you to think of. It's because the salesperson doesn't want you to see the competitor's price. It's because in the sanity of your kitchen, your old fridge seems just fine.

5. *Psychological debt.* Salespeople want you to start feeling that you owe them something. Lots of people try to get out of this by paying a compliment. "You do a really good job, but I'm not interested." Good salespeople refuse the compliment and turn it back on you: "No, if I was so good, I'd be taking your money right now. I'm not any good." Translation: "You still owe me. Don't you want to make me feel that I'm good? Help me. My kids are starving." Whatever. Don't give them anything.

Saying No

When you've got a debt crisis, it's okay to be rude to salespeople. It's probably okay anytime, for that matter. Simply walk away. Of course, it isn't that simple, or we wouldn't have the problems with consumer debt that we do. Here are some basics that can help.

1. *Shop two; decide at home.* For any purchase that requires a salesperson, be sure to "shop two; decide at home." We mentioned this in the credit counseling chapter, but it goes for any product or service. Banks? Cars? Lawyers? Shoes? Insurance? Psychics? Shop at two places and make your decision away from the salesperson. For one thing, you've automatically beaten the salesperson's urgency tactics, because you walked away. Tell salespeople that it's your rule. They will probably pull out every trick they know to keep you from walking out the door. That's a good sign that there is a better deal somewhere else, and they know it. Decide at home.

   At home, any other tactics are out of the way, too. Away from the bright lights, you can make an informed, thought-out decision based on facts, not the salesperson's personality or the picture of his or her skinny kids.

2. *Do your homework.* Any information you bring to the fray gives you an edge. Whether you're dealing with goods or services, a little pricing information puts you one up on the salesperson. The Internet provides a lot of places to get solid information on car costs for dealers. The paper will have sales you can brandish. Call other lawyers or insurance brokers for quotes before you talk to someone. Know at least something about what you're doing, and don't be afraid to call out a salesperson who stretches the truth.

3. *Make the salesperson convince you.* Ask questions like, "Why should I get this and not that?" "Will T.J. Maxx have these same shoes cheaper?" "Will the guy at Circuit City pressure me this way?" "What, besides your word, says that this is good advice?" Or anything else that forces the salesperson to be on the spot. Be skeptical and cynical and critical, even if you've always been a nice person before. Remember, salespeople laugh at nice people the minute they walk out of the store. They high-five and calculate their commission. Make them work for it. If you have any doubts, don't do it. Again, decide how convinced you are at home.

Saying No to Your family

Saying no to family is the most difficult thing there is. Isn't helping each other what a family is for? Well, yes. What's important to remember is that if you're having credit problems, then *you* are the one who needs help. Make that very clear, and don't feel bad about taking care of yourself.

You tried tough love, but it was just impossible? One person we know was about to go crazy over the way her grown son was asking her for money. She found it was impossible to say no until she found something similar to say. When he asked, she told him the exact amount she was in debt, explained that she was just about to call him for cash, asked him for fifty bucks every time he showed up because she was in so much trouble, and reminded him that helping each other was just what families were for. She never had to say no; she just asked first.

What's really useful from this woman's strategy is having numbers on hand. Demonstrate to any family member just how bad your situation is. If you have to, show them last month's electric bill and imply that it isn't paid yet. The truth is, you can help everyone much more by getting out of debt, not by being bled by people who are supposed to care. If you can't say no, show them why you have to first. It can help a lot.

Saying No to Charities (without Guilt)

The main concept here is, again, that if you are in big debt trouble, you are the charity. You truly can and will help them more when you are back on your financial feet. You should never feel bad about not helping when you need help as well. Think of it like this: Charities help the weak. It's better that you get strong and then help the weak to stand than to have two of you struggling in the dirt. If charities are important to you, then getting out of debt has to be, too. You can do so much more when you've got stress-free time and money to donate.

A second important point about charities is that not all charities are created equal. Be sure you're giving to an established cause with a good reputation. You'd be surprised how many scams there are out there. Do your research. And really, in this, like anything else, shop two and decide at home. Don't let a fundraiser try sales techniques on you. If you're interested, get his or her card and consider it alone in your living room, where you can better weigh your needs and your options.

Third, don't buy; donate and get a receipt.

For one thing, donations are tax-deductible (if it's a reputable non-profit), but if you simply buy something from the charity, it isn't. More importantly, donating ensures that 100 percent of your contribution goes to the charity and none of it goes to the salesperson.

Many charities have signed up with marketing firms. The way this works is, the salesperson comes to the door and asks you to play a game, the notorious "scratch-off" game. So you scratch a square, and underneath is an amount, say, seven bucks. So that's what you "help the program out with." In return, you get a sheet of coupons or some other nonsense. Make no mistake; you have just *bought* these coupons for $7. In the typical situation, the salesperson will keep one-third of that money. A little over a third goes to the marketing company, and 30 percent goes to the charity. In some places it's even worse. Even Christmas bell ringers have been known to be on commission with these firms.

It helps the charity, no doubt about it, because it doesn't have to do anything but sign on in order to start receiving money. However, it would receive a lot more money if you just sent it a donation of $7, and it would be tax-deductible for you.

Two of the salespeople we've met in this game drove brand-new Mercedes; one lived in a $300,000 house. All this from helping a non-profit "drug resistance" program. Further, this particular firm preyed on the poorest neighborhoods in the Los Angeles area because these neighborhoods were especially likely to be concerned about drugs. We never saw the sale fully explained to any Spanish speaker. Please, if you want to give, give to an organization directly; don't line the silk pockets of young fundraising salespeople.

And they are salespeople. Legally and literally. If one of these people comes to your house and says, "But I'm not selling anything," or if one of these people uses the word *give*, be sure to file a complaint with your local D.A. or the Federal Trade Commission (www.ftc.gov). It will say on whatever you get that "this is a purchase, not a donation." These people walk the very thin line that separates legal from scam. They must be certain not to step over that line.

Chapter 9

Special Problems

Getting out of debt and rebuilding your credit can sometimes involve addressing the special circumstances that got you into trouble in the first place. Most debt problems we encounter stem from consumers' living without an effective budget, but there are many who face situations that are not directly related to debt but that still manage to put them in the hole as a side effect.

Of course there are many more problems out there than we can adequately cover here, but we'll try to hit the major ones.

IDENTITY THEFT

Identity theft is the fastest-growing crime in America, and it's directly related to credit and debt issues. In most cases, identity thieves steal credit cards or social security numbers and open new accounts. This leaves you with wrecked credit and a lot of work ahead of you.

First of all, make sure that you haven't been a victim by checking your credit report regularly (see Chapter 6) and looking for any unfamiliar accounts or inquiries. Most of the time, the only way you'll be able to detect identity theft early will be by checking your own credit report.

If you have been a victim, start by calling 877-ID-THEFT (877-438-4338). This is the Federal Trade Commission's ID Theft Hotline; the FTC will take a statement from you and send you some useful information, including an "ID Theft Affidavit," which will be helpful in dealing with creditors who are trying to collect on fraudulent accounts.

Next, visit the FTC's identity theft web site at www.consumer. gov/idtheft. You'll get lots of helpful advice there.

With any case of identity theft, your first three steps will be these:

1. Contact the three major credit bureaus and report the theft. Don't use the contact information we gave you in Chapter 6 for this. The fraud departments have different numbers:
   a. Equifax: 1-800-525-6285
   b. Experian: 1-888-397-3742
   c. TransUnion: 1-800-680-7289
   Ask them to place a "fraud alert" on your file. Once you have done that, no new credit will be granted without your approval.
2. Contact the security departments of any creditors or financial institutions that hold accounts that were fraudulently accessed or opened. Report the theft and close the accounts immediately.
3. File a police report in the same jurisdiction in which the identity theft took place. You'll need the police report number or a copy of the report when dealing with creditors later.
   This is where you may run into some problems. Most likely, the police will not investigate the crime, and often they won't file a report at all. It's standard practice for many police departments to investigate cases of identity theft only when there is more than $50,000 in losses. What you really need from them is a letter confirming that you reported the crime. Sometimes you'll have to pester the police department to get this confirmation letter, but it's worth it if you have to deal with a creditor who wants more than your signed affidavit.
   Another common problem is that police reports generally must be filed in person. If someone commits the fraud in Anchorage, Alaska, and you live in Fife, Alabama, then it's not likely you'll be able to visit there any time soon. You'll have to work hard to get a police report filed in the place where the theft happened (Fife) instead of where the fraud happened (Anchorage).

In the case of fraudulent checks or credit card fraud, someone at the bank or credit card company will be assigned the case when you report it. Keep the number of the fraud investigator assigned to your case handy and give it to any collection agencies or defrauded creditors that continue to bother you.

If the collection agency absolutely insists on a police report, and the police absolutely refuse to accept it, contact your bank or credit card company to see if it was able to file a police report somewhere. Ultimately, it's the bank or creditor who was defrauded in a case of identity theft, because it was their money the thief spent. That's why the police may accept a report from them, since they can demonstrate a genuine financial loss. If you can get that police report number, then you should be able to use that when disputing the charge with a collector.

Another new approach police departments are taking is to issue a "Financial Crimes Report." This is like a police report except nothing is ever investigated or even considered for investigation. What it does is give you a document to use against collectors and a number that they can call for verification. An FCR, while it will never bring anyone to justice, might help you get some justice from those collection agencies.

Finally, remember that you may have to repeat this process if a new fraudulent account is discovered or a new fraudulent check is written. Even if the clerk at the police station knows you by heart and has your FCR ready for you every time you get through the line, you can never let up. You can be sure the thieves won't.

The good news is that you probably won't be held responsible for the fraudulent accounts. The bad news is that clearing your record of identity theft is time-consuming and potentially expensive. The best way to fight it is to detect it early by pulling your own credit reports regularly (once a year should do).

TAXES

We mentioned in Chapter 4 that you can offer the IRS a settlement on tax debt. That was perhaps a simplistic way to put it. There's an official process called an offer in compromise (OIC), and it has about a one in four chance of succeeding (statistically, the IRS rejects all but 23 percent of the OICs that it receives).

Because making an OIC is a risky proposition, you may want to hire a lawyer or a CPA to help you if you have significant tax debt. However, make sure you won't have to pay a large amount of money if your offer is rejected by the IRS; some professionals will want to charge you $2000 or more whether the OIC is accepted or not. Don't enter into that kind of agreement. A rejected OIC can be appealed, so stick with it until you have a final answer, and then pay only a fair amount for the work provided.

To submit an offer yourself, you need to complete IRS Form 656, plus Form 433-A, plus reams of supporting documentation—the IRS will know everything about your financial situation by the time you're done filing your OIC. This is bad, since it gives the IRS all the information it needs to collect the taxes you owe if your offer is rejected.

That's why you shouldn't submit an OIC unless it will be accepted. Of course there's no way to know for certain that it will be accepted, but we do know what the IRS is seeking. You need to prove that you meet one of the following conditions:

Doubt as to collectibility. The IRS won't be able to collect the tax bill now or in the foreseeable future.
Doubt as to liability. You don't actually owe the tax bill.

If your offer ends up being rejected, you can appeal or resubmit your offer. Usually you have to increase the amount you're offering to avoid being immediately rejected again.

FORECLOSURE

A foreclosure has multiple disastrous effects on your life: homelessness and ruined credit. And if your lender repossesses your house and can't sell it for more than you owe, you still have to pay the difference; the lender may get a deficiency judgment against you.

When you are facing this situation, stay in the house. If you abandon your property, you'll lose some of your rights. Communicate with your lender and try to work out an arrangement. There are several ways to avoid foreclosure:

Special forbearance. This is a repayment plan worked out between you and the lender. You have to disclose your personal financial information to show that you can make the new payments and that you deserve the assistance.

Mortgage modification. You can refinance the debt and possibly extend the term of your mortgage. You'll pay more in the long run, but your monthly payments will be reduced.

Partial claim. If you have an FHA loan that is between 4 and 12 months delinquent and you can resume full monthly payments, HUD may pay the delinquent amount for you from the FHA insurance fund. You'll have to pay the amount back (interest-free) when you either pay off the mortgage or sell the property.

Preforeclosure sale. If you can sell the house and get more money for it than you owe, you can escape the hardship of foreclosure. It's not as good as saving your home, but it beats having it forcibly taken from you.

Deed in lieu of foreclosure. You can give the house back to the lender voluntarily. You lose the house, but it's not as bad for your credit rating as foreclosure.

What Won't Work

1. *Equity skimming.* When you are facing foreclosure, don't deed your property to a third party. Some scam artists will offer to buy your property by selling it for you and paying off your mortgage. The scam involves your moving out of the house and signing your deed over to the fraudulent buyer. This person will rent it out and pocket the money until the lender forecloses, and you're the one who gets burned. Signing over your deed doesn't remove your obligation.

   This kind of scam is called "equity skimming," or sometimes "rent skimming." The scam artist is skimming because he or she is taking the income from your property and not using it to pay for or improve the home.

2. *Counseling agencies that charge fees.* This refers to fees for *housing* counseling, not credit counseling. HUD won't allow a counseling agency to charge you for housing counseling and keep its certification. Make sure that any housing counseling you get is free and that the counseling agency is HUD-certified.

   Whatever you do, don't sign anything that you don't fully understand, and check with your mortgage company or even a lawyer before entering into any kind of deal.

EVICTION

If you're a renter and you can't make the rent, eviction can begin, depending on your state's laws, as little as 1 day after the rent was due. The landlord will be required to give you notice that you must either pay or vacate in as few as 3 days. Again, all of this depends upon the laws of the state in which you live. Look for a local legal assistance provider and ask for advice.

In most states, if you don't have a lease or are renting month-to-month, a landlord can evict you for any reason. The best thing you can do is try to communicate with your landlord and work something out. If the landlord is intractable, you may want to look for a new place to live. You may be able to work out a deal with your landlord in which the landlord provides a reference for you in exchange for your agreement to move out and spare him or her an eviction battle.

Remember, you don't actually have to move out until a judge tells you to. Your landlord cannot legally change the locks, confiscate your stuff, or shut off your utilities. If the judge orders your eviction and you don't leave, a sheriff's deputy will show up and escort you off the premises.

If you've had money problems and your landlord just wants to be rid of you, she or he will probably be able to make it happen. Start shopping for a cheaper place.

AUTO REPOSSESSION

If your vehicle has been repossessed, the first thing you have to look at is the act of repossession. If the repo man harmed you or your property, he or she may be required to compensate you.

Also, repo men usually can't keep or sell personal property that they find in your car (depending on your state's laws). If they can't account for your personal property, you may be entitled to compensation.

You may be told what will happen to your car (in some states, this is a requirement). That way, you can bid on the car if there is a public auction. If the car is going to be sold to a private party, the institution that repossessed it may have to tell you the date of the sale.

Some states allow you to reclaim your car by paying the amount you owe plus the costs of repossession. That won't keep it from getting repossessed again if you fall behind in the future, though.

If the lender sells the car for less than you owe, you'll be expected to pay the difference. The lender will get a deficiency judgment against you from the court to make you pay. By law, though, the lender has to sell the car in a "commercially reasonable manner." What does that mean? For your purposes, it means that the lender can't give the car away for a pittance—it may not sell for much, but if you think the price was unreasonably low, you may have a claim against the lender, or at least a defense in court when the lender tries to have a deficiency judgment assigned to you.

If you lose, and you get a deficiency judgment, there's not much you can do except pay. Having won in court, the lender can garnish your wages if you don't. At this point, the best thing to do is to approach the lender and work out a repayment plan, or possibly offer a settlement.

The bottom line is, it's easier to prevent the repossession before it happens than to dispute it after the fact.

DIVORCE

This is a messy ordeal for most couples, and unfortunately one that can leave you with insurmountable debt. While a couple can divorce, their credit will stay married. If your ex files for bankruptcy, then you may have no choice but to follow suit.

If your divorce is reasonably amicable, try to separate your debt before you split up. The judge may order the husband to pay a particular credit card and the wife to pay another, but the credit card companies couldn't care less. They're still going to wreck both individuals' credit if one doesn't pay. The same applies to car loans, mortgages, lines of credit, and so on. Joint accounts will always be joint accounts, whether you're together or not.

Try to get new cards in each of your names and transfer balances to split up the debt. Then close any joint accounts. That way, the credit card company has only one target if payments on a particular card are missed. Try to do this with all your debts. Turn joint accounts into individual accounts. Talk to your divorce lawyer about negotiating this part of the split.

You may apply for individual consolidation loans to split up joint account balances as well. A clean break is what you're after; while that may not be possible with issues like child custody, it should be your goal as far as credit is concerned.

Some creditors may transfer the joint debt into one person's name if both of you approach them and request it, but they don't have to, and many won't. If your credit rating is good enough, get a new individual account right away so that you can have credit if your ex starts wreaking havoc.

Another thing to consider is the tax ramifications of a child custody decision. If you have more than one child and your divorce isn't too acrimonious, you might give at least one child to each spouse for tax reasons. That way both of you can file as a "head of household" with dependents and get a more favorable filing status.

Finally, you'll have your house to consider. It's usually a couple's most valuable asset, and you can't cut it in two. In many cases, selling it and splitting the proceeds is the best solution. Talk to your attorney about how to proceed.

MARRIAGE

When it comes to debt, *not* getting divorced can be a problem for consumers who are married to a compulsive debtor. You should follow much of the advice just given about your joint consumer accounts. If you separate your debt into individual accounts, at least one of you will have good credit.

Unfortunately, you won't be able to separate a mortgage, and ultimately, you will want to address the problem your spouse has with debt. Consider Debtors Anonymous if you can't come up with a solution on your own.

UNEMPLOYMENT

Unemployment has been on the rise lately; we recently saw 400 people apply for one open position. Whatever the reasons for your unemployment, you're not alone.

One small bit of good news is that unemployment compensation cannot be taken to pay debt. You should notify any collectors who have contacted you in writing that your income is exempt from garnishment. If they obtain a court judgment against you, they may try to seize your bank account. They can't do that if the money in the account came from unemployment compensation, but you may have to take legal action to protect your account.

Our best advice to the unemployed is to treat finding a job like a job in itself. Spend 40 hours a week job hunting and you're bound to find something.

Just as we've stressed throughout the book, you should communicate with your creditors and let them know your situation—they're likely to agree to help you find some way to ease your burden. This can be viewed as self-serving, since they really don't want you to file for bankruptcy, but the truth is that bankruptcy hurts everyone except bankruptcy attorneys, so you can accept your creditors' assistance in good faith.

INSURANCE

No, this section won't teach you how to commit insurance fraud to repay your debts. In fact, we'll tell you one of the principal reasons why that won't work.

We've mentioned car salespeople as individuals not to be trusted. Well, if car salespeople are enemy number one, then enemy number two would be insurance claims adjusters.

Adjusters—and anyone who works for the insurance company, for that matter—have one job (and one job only): to avoid paying claims. They don't want to help you, they aren't on your side, and no matter how nice they are to you, their job is to find a way not to pay your claim. It's as simple as that.

You can see that getting away with fraud can be complicated. If you try it, you'll get caught, because the adjuster is going to be looking awfully hard for any evidence that will excuse the company from paying you a dime.

Unfortunately, the company will try to avoid paying your honest claims, too. You have to have all your ducks in a row to win against these folks. Of course you'll get your settlement if you deserve it, but the company will do what it can to reduce the amount paid to you.

As for the costs of insurance, you should definitely shop around to find the best rate; they vary widely, and it's not difficult to find a better rate if you shop thoroughly. The problem is, the lower your rate, the more likely the insurance company is to fight you when you file a claim. It can afford to charge less because it's paying fewer claims than its competitors.

These days, many consumers are saving money on insurance by going with large companies that operate without local insurance agents. You can pay less because the company doesn't have to pay someone to have an office in your neighborhood. You usually have to apply for insurance with these companies by phone or via the Internet, since they won't have a face-to-face office near you.

But is this in your best interest? Are you better off having an agent with whom you can build a relationship? That's a matter of personal preference, really. Just make sure that you choose a licensed company with no complaints with the Better Business Bureau or your state's insurance board.

Besides the costs of insurance, your credit will affect whether you can get coverage in some circumstances. Some insurance companies consider policyholders with low FICO scores to be a higher insurance risk and deny or discontinue their coverage. This is yet another reason to manage your debt wisely and establish the best credit rating you can.

UTILITY SHUTOFF/PHONE DISCONNECTION

In most cases, utility companies won't rush to shut off your service if you miss a payment. It can take several months for them to turn off your service if they can't collect what they're owed. And in colder parts of the country, they won't turn the heat off during the winter months. That's one thing that complicates this issue: It varies from state to state. Contact your nearest legal assistance agency if you've received a shutoff notice.

Also, bear in mind that it's much easier to avoid shutoff than to have your service restored. This goes for the utility company as well as for you. Talk to the company about your options; it should offer you some way to keep your service by paying installments or direct you to an assistance outlet.

As for telephone service, the phone company is much more likely to shut off service quickly if you don't pay your phone bill. There was a time when this could be devastating, since you couldn't get new phone service anywhere until you paid your bill.

But the proliferation of cellular phones has made it easier to get some kind of phone service if yours is disconnected. You can get prepaid cell phone services these days, which means that the cell phone company won't turn you down because you have bad credit, so phone disconnection is more of a nuisance than a serious problem.

UNEXPECTED EMERGENCIES

By their very definition, unexpected emergencies cannot be completely prepared for. The best thing you can do is budget wisely and build your emergency savings fund to deal with emergency situations when they occur.

You'll also want insurance to protect you from natural disasters and theft. Even if you're a renter, you need insurance. It doesn't cost much, and it will be worth it if anything happens to your property.

Remember that the people who work for your creditors have the same problems as the rest of us, and they can be understanding if you explain your situation to them. They'll get tired of hearing excuses month after month, but if your emergency is an isolated incident, you can expect them to offer you some relief from your payment schedule. This goes for all kinds of debt: Even mortgage loan payments can be safely skipped or deferred under certain circumstances.

HOLIDAY SPENDING

First of all, gift giving may be great, but it's almost never essential. Don't make a bad situation worse by giving extravagant gifts when you can't afford to pay your bills. And don't shop for holiday gifts with credit cards if you aren't prepared to pay the balance in full by the end of the month.

In fact, try to avoid using credit cards at all when shopping for the holidays. They create too much of a temptation to overspend, and there are lots of things that we simply won't buy if we have to part with cold, hard cash to get them. Besides, credit isn't free, and you have to factor its cost into the cost of the gift. It's better to pay cash and pay full price than to buy an item on sale with a credit card.

The holidays should be planned for in advance. If you can save the money to buy gifts, knock yourself out. Make the holidays an annual savings goal: Decide what you want to spend well in advance, and work toward that amount.

One way to make that happen is to make a list of everyone you want to buy for and what you plan to spend. Planning in advance can really help you avoid overspending. Make sure to include the cost of decorations, wrapping paper, and so on, so that all holiday spending is included.

Some people get a part-time job during the holidays just to pay for their holiday spending. It's easy enough to find seasonal work in retail shops if you want to go that way.

The key is to set the right priorities. You may be embarrassed to buy less expensive gifts for your loved ones for fear of letting them know that you're experiencing financial difficulty. You have to get over that. If they're truly your loved ones, they won't want to see you overextend yourself just to impress them. You can always give to charity in their names and give your friends and family a card saying that a donation was made on their behalf. That's what the holidays are really about, anyway.

KIDS AND CHILD-CARE EXPENSES

There is a great deal of help available on child-care spending, in the form of both information and actual money. Be sure to find out about every possible assistance program that might be able to help you out. You can start by contacting your state's department of social services. If there are federal programs you qualify for, your state agency will help you find those, too.

Often this agency can point you to better or cheaper child care, even if for some reason it can't help you pay for it. Ask around about co-ops, too. The women in the social services department where we live are a clearinghouse of "mom" information.

A second important step is to keep track of every penny that has to do with raising your kid, for tax reasons. Tax relief is the first relief for parents. You get an additional exemption and a new child tax credit; this is worth approximately $1300 per year for a middle-income family. Parents who use day care get an additional $480 in savings. These days many employers have flexible spending accounts that can save you money in this area. Check with your human resources person to find out what your company offers.

If you really want some good advice on keeping kid costs low while you manage a debt problem, the best resource is an experienced mom in your neighborhood. Try to find one with three kids or more—the more the better. She will know all the hot spots for money-saving deals, where to go, and precisely when. Not only that, she'll be a great reality check, too. When you're looking at the designer stuff, she can set you straight. Ask someone with kids entering college what they would have done differently. Prepare for the wicked laugh, but scribble down the advice.

Finally, there are plenty of cheesy but helpful sites on the Web that collect money-saving tips. "Ron and Debbie's Penny Pinchin' Kids Page" is a fine example.

Two Quick Tips for Parents

1. Every baby product sports a 1-800 number for questions or comments, but if you call it, you can usually get some coupons just for asking.
2. Buy the classics, whether it's clothes or toys. The hottest thing gets cold; the blue chips have hand-me-down and resale value. Try selling a Teddy Ruxpin at a garage sale and he'll end up at the Goodwill by the end of the day, but old Legos will be gone before lunch.

SINGLE PARENTS

Being a single parent is a tough situation for obvious reasons. There are a couple of specific things that single parents must consider. The first is estate planning. Because there is no one else to make decisions about your kids and your money when you're gone, you must make those decisions now. A will ensures that everything you own will get to your children efficiently and in the way you specify. It's also important for naming your children's guardians. If you don't have a legal will and something happens, the state will make these decisions instead of you. Unfortunately, most states are not so good at this. It's always much better to do it yourself.

The second issue that single parents must consider as soon as possible is college planning. This goes for all parents—even two-parent households have trouble paying for college—but single parents have to play perfectly in order to win this game.

Start early and get good advice from a financial adviser you trust. Find out what other parents did that worked and what failed, and make your decisions accordingly. One thing that's important is to keep the college funds in your own name. Having major assets can hurt a kid's chances of getting grants or other types of financial aid. Not only that, but a custodial account that is turned over to the child at age 18 can be a problem if for some reason the child doesn't want to use it for college. It's better if you hold on to that money for a while. A lot of people decide that college is a good idea a few years later.

We would also strongly suggest the Section 529 savings plan. This is a government program that lets your child's college money grow without being taxed. There are probably other options, too; just be sure you talk to someone who knows them all, and then talk to someone else. As with any other service, when it comes to financial advisers and your child's future, shop several and weigh the advice at home. Then make your decision.

Don't stop looking for other sources of financial advice. There is an abundance of inspiring stories out there about single mothers who made it. You might check out www.singleMOMZ.com for some advice about almost everything. Remember, as a single parent, you get to make all the decisions, but you take all the responsibility, too. Be well researched. You've got to be.

THE TRUE COST OF SMOKING

Forget about the health risk; this is a book about debt. For all Thom knows, the stress he's relieved through smoking would have killed him faster than the cigarettes. But we do know this: Even though Thom smokes less than a pack a day and always bargain-shops, in the past 7 years he's spent approximately $6300 on cigarettes. If he'd put that money against one of his credit cards, he'd have saved an additional 900 bucks. And if he could invest that $7200 in an IRA right now, he would have over $25,000 in extra cash by the time he retires.

Think of it: 25 grand. Enough for a new truck, not enough for a lung transplant. That's the true cost of smoking.

WOMEN PAYING MORE

Oh, sure, let's add to the list of ways our society mistreats women. Well, it's not as bad as you've always been told, but there are some iniquities in our system that tend to lead women to spend more than they should.

And we're not talking about cosmetics and manicures. There are plenty of things men spend money on that women don't. (It's not women who are calling those phone sex hotlines, is it?) What we're talking about is debt.

The average client in credit counseling is female, around 30, perhaps with a child. Does that suggest that single mothers are more likely to have debt problems than men? Not really; it only suggests that women are more likely to seek help than men.

And that's true of married women as well. Credit counselors will frequently see female clients who come in on behalf of themselves and their husbands. Just as they are less likely to stop to ask for directions when they are lost, men in our culture are less likely to reach out than women.

But since women are our largest client demographic and they have special issues to address, we feel it's important to offer some special advice to them.

Gender-Biased Pricing

Some things are marketed "for women only," but aren't any different from the similar products for men and cost three times as much. Check out the equivalent men's product and see if you can really detect a difference. Shaving cream for men will work just as well on your legs as it does on our faces, and it won't cost you as much. If we haven't bred a thorough distrust of advertising in you by now, we've failed (or you haven't read the whole book).

On top of that, women's clothing is more likely to have to be dry-cleaned than men's, hair stylists cost more than barbers, and men don't need gynecologists. Being a woman is just more expensive. Sorry, ladies, you need a budget more than anyone.

The Myth of 69 Cents on the Dollar

While we're on the subject, yes, it's more expensive to be a woman, but all that stuff you hear about women making 69 cents for every dollar a man earns is misleading.

Yes, women earn less than men, but not for the same work. Men and women make the same pay for the same jobs. The problem is, historically female occupations (nurses, teachers, flight attendants, clerical workers) pay less than historically male occupations. And men dominate the upper management departments in most companies. This is unfortunate and wrong, but the women who do get to upper management are generally paid the same as their male colleagues.

This is a complicated issue, and we're not going to settle it here to anyone's satisfaction. The bottom line is, women do earn less than men in our society, and that presents special problems for women who want to conquer debt and build good credit.

The Truth about Car Salespeople

We've warned you not to trust car salespeople (or any other kind of salespeople, for that matter), and this is particularly important if you're female. Statistically, car dealerships make more profit from women than they do from men. Salespeople try to make the most profit for themselves, and they're going to exploit every perceived advantage that they've got. And for many a car salesperson (a sexist lot, they are), that means charging women more.

Their thinking is that women know less about cars than men, and so they won't know when they're being taken advantage of. Auto dealerships tend to be less flexible when dealing with women than when dealing with men.

This goes for other professions as well. Plumbers, auto mechanics, contractors, and so on—they all tend to charge women more than they charge men for the same work.

What can you do about it? For one thing, get tough. If you know the fair price for the product or service, demand it. If you don't know the fair price, find out what it is from an objective source or by comparison shopping. Find someone who does know about cars—male or female—to assist you in your negotiations. Use a car-buying service provided by your credit union or auto club. Whatever you do, don't let a crooked salesperson get the best of you.

And stick together. Get a recommendation from another woman if you're looking for a mechanic you can trust. You may even want to do the same when choosing a doctor, since studies have shown that doctors order more tests for women than for men with the same symptoms. (This may be justified, given the differences in physiology between the genders, but it can't hurt to get a second opinion.)

All this stuff adds up to debt for females in our society. Not to mention the narrow and impossible standards of beauty imposed by the culture that are expensive for those who aspire to them. And the culture deliberately tries to turn women into "shoppers"; there's even a Barbie doll with her own credit card.

Remember these tenets about shopping:

Shopping isn't entertainment. It's what you do to get the things you need. If shopping is your idea of a good time, find a cheaper hobby.

Shopping won't cure your depression. Address what's really causing your depressed feelings. We doubt that "I didn't do enough shopping" will make it into your suicide note.

Discounts are meaningless if you weren't already planning the purchase. Don't buy things you don't need just because they're on sale. Junk bought at discount prices is just cheap junk.

Debt is no reward. People may purchase things they don't need as a small reward to themselves for doing something good. But if you buy with credit, you've really punished yourself with debt and interest and fees and lasting headaches. Don't reward yourself by spending money you haven't earned yet.

You need a budget. This applies to men, women, and everything in between. It's a basic survival skill, not an onerous burden.

Chapter 10

Breaking the Cycle: What to Tell Your Children

Just about every parent shares the same goal: to see their children live a better life than they did. If you have kids, it's important to teach them how to handle debt responsibly.

IT'S YOUR JOB: WHY PARENTS, NOT SCHOOLS, HAVE TO TEACH FINANCIAL LITERACY

Traditionally, parents have always been responsible for teaching their children how to manage their money. In the old days, it was common for parents to take a child to the bank to help him or her set up his or her first account. Children learned to count and add in school, but Mom and Dad handed down the wisdom and common sense.

Times have changed. These days, kids are raised in single-parent homes more than ever. And in two-parent homes, both parents have to work so that the family can get by.

These days, schools are teaching your kids to stay off drugs, be tolerant, practice safe sex, recycle, and so on, in addition to reading, writing, and arithmetic. So many things that used to be the responsibility of the parent have been passed on to schools that kids are learning less than ever.

Parents have to step up and prepare their children to leave the nest. They're not going to learn financial literacy in school; they've got to learn it at home.

Jump$tart Coalition and Other Efforts

There are organizations like EdFund and NEFE (National Endowment for Financial Education), among others, that are dedicated to teaching kids about financial literacy. Most prominent among them is probably the Jump$tart Coalition (www.jumpstart.org).

Jump$tart surveys high school graduates every few years to see how financially literate they are. Unfortunately, since Jump$tart has come into being, students' scores on financial literacy have plummeted.

Is Jump$tart failing? It's hard to say. It does a good job of preparing surveys, but it hasn't yet done much to actually educate students. The Jump$tart movement is still young, and given time, it may effect some change. But for now, realize that financial literacy among our students has been dropping steadily for a decade.

Our position is that it's the parents who have to be educated about financial literacy, and that they should be the ones to pass that knowledge on to their kids. We can't rely on other organizations or our schools to do that work.

THINGS KIDS HAVE TO LEARN

- *You have to work before you get paid.* As educators, we can tell you that nothing is worse than a child who doesn't understand this concept, except perhaps an adult who doesn't understand this concept. We're not suggesting that you become a slave driver, but create a system of chores for your children and tie those chores to their allowance. Start young. The chores can be as simple as putting their toys away, and the allowance can be a nickel, but as long as you create a relationship between the two, you're succeeding.
- *Credit unions are better than piggy banks.* Financial institutions are the place to keep your money, not under the mattress. Take your child to a bank or credit union that offers custodial

accounts. A decent financial institution will open an account for a child of any age with the parent as the custodian. If the bank says it doesn't offer custodial accounts, take your business elsewhere; it's a shortsighted institution that doesn't see the value of developing future banking customers, and it deserves the failure that it will eventually face. Remember to keep the college fund somewhere separate and under your name, though. Too many assets in your child's name can damage her or his ability to qualify for grants or financial aid.

- *Saving is important.* Teach your child to always put something away for a rainy day. You should lead by example in this case. There is very little in our culture that is going to encourage children to save, and saving is a vital part of overall financial health.
- *Sound money management ≠ greed.* The goal isn't to hoard money or to become materialistic to the point of obsession. Caring about one's financial well-being doesn't mean that one has to act like Ebenezer Scrooge. Teach children the importance of tipping, donating to charity, and gift giving. It's all part of the equation.
- *Budgeting is important.* Just as you should have a plan for spending your money, so should your kids. Impulse buying is a bad habit to develop. If your child sees something that he or she wants to purchase, help him or her set a savings goal and put aside money from his or her allowance until enough has been saved up to purchase it. If your child still wants the item by the time the money has been saved, then the child can get it.
- *Don't wait.* The earlier one starts saving, the better. Kids should be saving for college from the day they enter preschool. They should be saving for retirement from the day they finish high school. However you calculate it, the cost of waiting to start savings is jaw-dropping.
- *All income should go to the bank.* Whether it's the regular weekly allowance, money earned from specific chores, or a birthday gift from Grandma, it should be treated the same way. Encourage anyone who gives money to your children to do it in check form; that way, the child has to take the money to the bank. This is a valuable learning experience and discourages impulse spending. That

goes for you, too. Don't dole out that allowance in cash; write your child a check instead.

INVOLVING YOUR KIDS IN THE FAMILY FINANCES

Include your kids in the family budgeting and bill-paying processes. This will teach them crucial lessons about financial responsibilities. Your kids will be likely to demand less of you if they understand your family's financial realities. And your teenagers need to know what those long-distance phone calls do to your phone bill.

THE FIRST, BEST TOOL: PUT THEM ON AN ALLOWANCE

We've been talking as if the allowance is a given. It is. If you want your children to become truly financially literate, then you *must* set up an allowance for them. Start early; some experts suggest starting as early as age 3.

Make the allowance weekly, and tie it to the child's household obligations. We know many parents who don't believe kids should have to work; we also know many adults who don't think they should have to work. Coincidence? Hardly. We're not saying that you should send them to the salt mines, but if they take out the garbage, load the dishwasher, and clean their own room, then they've earned their allowance.

How much to give? Give them their age. A 5-year-old gets 5 bucks a week. By the time they're teenagers, they could be earning a respectable amount of money (and helping more around the house: mowing the lawn, washing the car, and so on). The concept of "a raise" is a good one to impart, and understanding it from an early age will serve your children well throughout their adulthood.

No advances—if the allowance is spent, it's spent. They don't get next week's allowance until next week. They're not going to have an easy time getting payroll advances in their adult life, so don't get them started down that path now.

Do not withhold the allowance as a punishment. If the child didn't *earn* it this week, fine. But if you dock a child's allowance for misbehaving in school, you've just taught her or him that it's possible to buy your way out of trouble. Bad lesson.

Obviously, you won't make your children pay for everything. You'll still keep them fed and clothed, and a percentage of their allowance isn't going to add up to an acceptable college savings fund. What they need to be paying for are the toys, games, CDs, dates, and any other nonessential things that they want. The college fund that they started when they were 5 will be theirs to spend on the extra expenses of college life. If they've been saving that money for 15 years, they'll be less likely to blow it on beer and pizza.

CHILD DEVELOPMENT AND MONEY—ADVICE FOR EVERY AGE GROUP

0 to 4 years: Involve your children in household chores. At the very least, make sure they pick up their toys and put them away. Don't give them money for it yet—get them used to helping out without expecting to be paid for it. You should, however, let them play with money appropriately if they're curious about it.

4 to 5 years: Begin giving your children a small allowance each week, and make sure they set a portion of that aside in savings and, depending on your priorities, for charity. (If you want to teach your children to tithe, then it's especially crucial that you focus on money with them from an early age.) Begin teaching them basic rules about money, like cash transactions and banking. Periodically, as their piggy bank fills up, take them to the bank to deposit their savings in their own bank account.

5 to 6 years: Change the weekly allowance to incorporate the tasks your children are expected to complete. It's appropriate to dock a portion of their allowance if they don't fulfill their household obligations. It's important to make a strong connection between work and pay, but you shouldn't make it personal.

7 to 8 years: Now is the time to begin giving your children more power over how they spend their own money, but they'll need gentle guidance about savings goals. Help them understand when birthdays and holidays are approaching and it's important for them to set aside some of their allowance. Matching a child's savings might be an appropriate way to help them make a purchase without simply giving them everything they want.

9 to 11 years: You can start teaching your children about more advanced concepts now, like compound interest. Go through the paperwork on their savings account (they'd better have one by now!) and show them how saving can earn them extra money. This is also a good time to stress saving for college, if you haven't already. (Of course a child probably won't be able to commit much money to a college fund on a preteen allowance; encouraging the habit of saving is more important than the actual amount of money accrued.)

12 to 16 years: Your children can now be responsible for their own spending decisions. If you've taught them to save and have them on an allowance, then many of the typical burdens of parenting a teen can be lessened. Of course your teen wants to wear make-up and have expensive clothes, but you're under no obligation to buy them. We're not suggesting that you become an ogre, but if your kid wants a $50 pair of jeans when a $20 pair will suffice, then he or she is going to have to foot the extra $30. See how that works? Your children have to make choices, and if they can't afford everything they want, then they need to budget smarter. At any rate, it won't be your fault.

Of course something big is coming up: sweet 16. Will your child have a car? Will she or he pay for a portion of it? What about gas and insurance? Good luck. Maybe you should consider getting an old VW Bug from the junkyard and giving it to your 15-year-old along with a toolkit and a Chilton manual. If the kid can get it running by the time he or she is 16, the kid has a car. At least then your child will know something about automotive maintenance and will be able to do some of the repairs (and be less helpless when the car breaks down, less likely to get ripped off by an unscrupulous mechanic, and so on).

16 to 18 years: Now is the time for summer jobs and part-time work. If your children want to have that car and go out with friends, then they can work to pay for it. You've taught them the value of a dollar, and they should understand by now that nothing comes free. If all has gone well, they'll be making sound money choices and maintaining their savings.

18 and up: They're all grown up, like it or not. It's time to stop the weekly allowance and let them fend for themselves. They should be fine if you've taught them to manage their money well. You can keep helping them if they're in college and can't earn enough on the side to get by, but the weekly allowance will be over. They can also make some decisions about their college fund now, too.

Another thing that you might as well take care of now is their first credit card. If they don't have one at 18, they're going to get one soon. You might as well help them get it and manage it wisely. Don't let them carry balances from month to month, and stress to them that one credit card is all any consumer needs. Our advice to college students without credit is to get a gas card and use it only at the pump. It's a small, manageable expense that can be paid off monthly, and it will go a long way toward establishing good credit if they handle it responsibly.

Whatever you do to teach your kids about money, it's crucial that you lead by example. You can't expect your children to be good stewards of their money when you don't manage yours well.

Index

About the Authors

Jeff Michael is the Director of Education for Springboard Non-Profit Consumer Credit Management. He has personally taught thousands of consumers how to rebuild their credit and establish budgets effectively.

Thom Fox is a writer and educator living in Kansas City, Missouri. Together with Jeff, he has written plays that have been produced across the United States.